I0459200

Why I Love Being in Love with Myself

A Bold Guide to Choosing Yourself Every Day

By: Bridgette Gajadhar

Why I Love Being in Love With Myself

A Bold Guide to Choosing Yourself Every Day
By: Bridgette Gajadhar

Published by: Pons Veritas™
ISBN: 978-1-968471-01-9

www.ponsveritas.com

Disclaimer

This book is for informational and personal development purposes only. The content reflects the author's experiences, insights, and perspectives and is not intended as professional, medical, psychological, financial, or legal advice. Readers are encouraged to do their own research and seek guidance from qualified professionals where necessary. The author and

Table of Contents

Introduction

Let's get one thing straight—self-love is not a trend. It's not bubble baths, expensive skincare, or some aesthetic you curate for Instagram. It's not an excuse to be selfish or a way to prove something to anyone. Self-love is the foundation. The blueprint. The only relationship you're guaranteed to have for life. So why wouldn't you make it the best one?

Most people think they love themselves... until life tests them. Until someone treats them like an afterthought, and they accept it. Until they're faced with failure, and their inner voice sounds more like a bully than a best friend. Until they look in the mirror and can't stand the reflection. That's when you realize self-love isn't just a cute concept—it's survival.

Here's the truth: The way you love yourself sets the tone for everything in your life. Your relationships, your success, your peace, your energy—it all starts with you. Because when you truly love yourself, you stop tolerating things that drain, diminish, or disrespect you. You stop seeking validation from people who wouldn't even validate a parking ticket. You stop living life as a background character in someone else's story.

This book isn't here to tell you to "just love yourself" and move on. You've heard that before, and it clearly wasn't enough. This book is here to reset everything you thought you knew about self-love and show you what it really means. How to build it. How to apply it. How to let it transform every single part of your life.

Self-love is more than a mindset—it's an energy. It's that quiet confidence that doesn't need to announce itself. It's the way you move, the way you think, the way you choose yourself—every single day.

And if you're ready to unlock that? To step into the version of yourself that doesn't just survive but thrives? Then let's begin.

Before We Begin: A Self-Love Check-In

Before we dive into this journey, let's take a moment to be **real** with ourselves. No filters. No sugarcoating. Just **raw honesty**. Because self-love starts with **awareness**—knowing where you are, so you can decide where you want to go.

Take a deep breath. Exhale. And answer these questions **for you.** Not for how you *think* you should feel, but for how you **actually** feel.

1. How do you speak to yourself?

Would you talk to your best friend the way you talk to yourself? Do your thoughts lift you up, or do they tear you down?

Positive Example: "I encourage myself. I remind myself that I am capable, worthy, and growing."

Negative Example: "I criticize myself constantly. I always feel like I'm not enough."

2. What do you tolerate in your life that you know you shouldn't?

What habits, relationships, or situations drain you but you *still* allow? Why?

3. When was the last time you truly put yourself first?

Not in a "treat yourself" way, but in a **deep, meaningful way**—choosing your peace, setting a boundary, saying *no* without guilt.

4. Do you trust yourself?

When your gut tells you something, do you listen? Or do you second-guess yourself, seek validation, or let fear talk you out of it?

5. How do you define your worth?

Is your self-worth based on achievements? Looks? What others think? Or is it something **solid**—something no one can take away?

6. What's one thing you wish you could change about how you treat yourself?

If you could instantly shift **one** thing about how you show up for yourself, what would it be?

Now, Take a Moment.

Look at your answers. No judgment. Just **awareness.** Because this book isn't about *forcing* you to love yourself overnight. It's about **understanding yourself first.**

Self-love is a process. A journey. And this check-in? It's your starting point.

By the end of this book, you won't just answer these questions differently. You'll **feel** different. Move different. **Love yourself different.**

So if you're ready to **upgrade your entire energy**—let's begin.

Part 1: The Foundation – Loving Yourself as You Are

Let's start with the **truth**—real, unfiltered, and undeniable.

You don't have to "earn" self-love. You don't have to hit a goal, fix yourself, or become some perfect version of who you think you *should* be before you deserve to love yourself. **You are worthy, right now, exactly as you are.**

But here's where most people get stuck: They mistake self-love for an *end goal*—something you unlock **after** you become successful, look a certain way, or have everything figured out. But that's backwards. Self-love isn't the **reward**—it's the **foundation.** It's what helps you *become* that successful, happy, thriving version of yourself.

Because the truth is, the way you see yourself **affects everything.** Your relationships. Your confidence. The way you handle setbacks. The way you show up in life. If you don't believe you're worthy, you'll settle. You'll accept less than what you deserve. You'll keep waiting for permission to feel good about yourself instead of **choosing** to feel good about yourself.

And that stops *here*.

This section is about **getting real with yourself**—who you are, how you treat yourself, and what's been holding you back from *fully* embracing your worth. We're diving deep into the **mindset shifts** that will change everything, because self-love isn't just a *feeling*—it's how you **think, move, and operate.**

We're covering:

What self-love really is (and what it isn't).

How to stop waiting for external validation and start loving yourself for *existing*.

Breaking bad mental habits that keep you stuck in self-doubt.

Tuning into your intuition and trusting yourself unapologetically.

The power of your words and how what you say about yourself *shapes your reality*.

This is the work that makes everything else possible. This is the reset. This is how you build a love so solid within yourself that no rejection, failure, or outside opinion can shake it.

Because when you **love yourself as you are,** you move differently. You stop chasing and start attracting. You stop proving and start existing. You stop surviving and start *thriving*.

Let's get into it.

Chapter 1: What Is Self-Love, Really?

Let's Clear This Up: Self-Love Isn't What You Think

Let's get one thing straight—self-love is **not** arrogance. It's **not** selfishness. It's **not** perfection. And it's **definitely not** just an aesthetic you put on for social media.

Self-love is **self-acceptance. Self-mastery**. It's knowing yourself, respecting yourself, and choosing yourself—even when no one else does.

A lot of people think they love themselves, but what they really love is the **version** of themselves that's performing. The version that's productive, that looks good, that people praise. But what happens when you're not achieving? When you're not looking your best? When no one is hyping you up?

That's when **real** self-love shows itself. Because self-love isn't just about celebrating the best parts of yourself—it's about embracing **all** of yourself, even on the days when you don't feel like much.

Think about a time when you felt unworthy. Maybe you made a mistake, felt rejected, or weren't at your best. How did you treat yourself in that moment? Did you offer yourself kindness, or did you turn on yourself?

If your love for yourself disappears when things aren't perfect, that's **not** self-love. That's conditional self-acceptance—and we're here to break free from that.

Self-Love vs. Self-Care: Know the Difference

People love to mix these up. **Self-care** is a practice. **Self-love** is a mindset.

Self-care is taking a break, booking the massage, having a solo date night. It's doing things that nourish your body and mind. **It's important, but it's just one piece of the puzzle.**

Self-love is deeper. It's the way you **think**, the way you **treat yourself**, and the way you **show up** for yourself daily.

Because here's the truth: **You can do all the self-care in the world, but if you don't genuinely love yourself, you'll still feel empty.**

- You can take the **bubble bath**, but if your inner voice is still saying, *I'm not enough*, the water won't wash that away.
- You can buy the **designer bag**, but if your self-worth is tied to material things, the glow won't last.
- You can post **cute selfies with affirmations**, but if you don't actually believe them, they're just words.

Too many people use self-care as a temporary escape instead of a tool for deep self-love. **Real self-love isn't about escaping your life—it's about creating a life you don't need to escape from.**

Because let's be real—self-care can feel good in the moment, but if you're not doing the **inner work**, you're just putting a band-aid on a deeper wound. You can meditate, light candles, and do face masks every night, but if your self-talk is still toxic, the glow will only last until reality hits again.

Self-care is **external actions**.

Self-love is **internal transformation**.

Self-care is an **important tool**, but self-love is the **foundation**. And when you truly love yourself, self-care stops feeling like something you "have to" do and becomes something you naturally **want** to do—because you genuinely value yourself.

So don't just treat yourself like a queen for a day. **Commit to treating yourself like royalty every day.** Period.

Self-care is a tool to support self-love, but it's not a substitute for doing the inner work.

What Self-Love Looks Like vs. What People Think It Is

So many people mistake **performative self-love** for the real thing. They think it's about flexing on their ex, posting thirst traps, or cutting off everyone who disagrees with them.

And while those things might feel good in the moment, **they're not the foundation of real self-love.**

Things That Seem Like Self-Love (But Aren't):

- **Buying expensive things to prove your worth.** (*True self-worth doesn't need a price tag.*) It's one thing to enjoy luxury, but if you're constantly spending to prove something—to yourself or others—ask yourself why. Self-love isn't about looking rich, it's about **knowing you're valuable even without material validation.**

- **Seeking validation from others constantly.** (*If you don't validate yourself first, outside approval will never be enough.*) Selfies and compliments are cute, but if your confidence is built on how many likes or comments you get, it will crumble the second you don't get them. True self-love means **feeling worthy even when no one is clapping for you.**

- **Only loving yourself when you look good.** (*Self-love isn't conditional—it's an always thing.*) If your confidence disappears when you have a bad hair day, gain a little weight, or don't feel "on," that's not self-love—it's self-approval based on appearance. Real self-love is **loving yourself through every version of you**, not just the polished one.

- **Cutting people off without self-reflection.** (*Boundaries are necessary, but growth comes from understanding why you attract certain people.*) Yes, protecting your energy is key. But if you keep cutting off people without looking at your own patterns, you're avoiding growth. Real self-love **means taking accountability** for what you allow into your life and learning from your experiences—not just running from them.

- **Avoiding discomfort instead of healing.** (*Healing is messy. Self-love means facing what you've been avoiding, not running from it.*) Healing doesn't always feel good. In fact, it can be **uncomfortable, painful, and exhausting**. But running away from emotions, distracting yourself, or suppressing what needs to be addressed isn't self-love—it's avoidance. Real self-love is **choosing to do the work**, even when it's hard.

None of these things are **bad** on their own, but they **don't create real confidence**. They're **surface-level actions** that might bring temporary satisfaction, but they won't build the **deep, unshakable self-love** that lasts through every season of life.

What Real Self-Love Looks Like:
- **Respecting yourself even when no one is watching.** (*You don't need an audience to treat yourself with care.*) Your true character isn't in what you do when people are watching—it's in what you do **when no one's around.** Do you keep your promises to yourself? Do you take care of your mind and body because you love yourself, not because someone else is looking? Real self-love is about **honoring yourself in private, not just in public.**
- **Forgiving yourself for past mistakes and learning from them.** (*Growth comes from grace, not self-punishment.*) You're not perfect. You've made mistakes. **Welcome to being human.** Holding onto guilt and shame doesn't make you a better person—it just keeps you stuck. Self-love is about **giving yourself the same grace you'd give to someone you care about** and using those lessons to grow.
- **Trusting yourself to make the right decisions.** (*Doubt fades when you learn to trust your own judgment.*) If you're always second-guessing yourself or waiting for someone else to validate your choices, you're giving away your power. Self-love is about **building self-trust—** knowing that you are capable of making decisions that serve you, even if no one else agrees.

- **Sacrificing temporary comfort for long-term growth.** (*Not everything that feels good is good for you.*) Real self-love means being willing to do the hard things that help you grow. Whether it's breaking a toxic cycle, stepping out of your comfort zone, or committing to something meaningful, **growth requires discomfort.** Choosing long-term fulfillment over short-term pleasure is one of the deepest acts of self-respect.

- **Committing to your own happiness and well-being.** (*Not in a selfish way, but in a self-respecting way.*) This isn't about ignoring others—it's about **not abandoning yourself** in the process of loving others. True self-love means **prioritizing your own happiness** so that you can show up fully in every area of your life.

- **Supporting yourself through highs and lows.** (*Even on bad days, you deserve your own love.*) Loving yourself on good days is easy. But what about the days when you feel like a mess? When you fail? When you disappoint yourself? **That's when self-love matters most.** It's about standing by yourself, just like you would for a close friend, even when things aren't pretty.

- **Setting and achieving goals that align with your purpose.** (*Not what looks good to others—what feels right for you.*) Are you chasing goals because you actually want them, or because they sound impressive? Self-love is about **living for YOU**, not for validation, clout, or expectations. If it doesn't bring you joy, why are you doing it?

- **Growing into the best version of yourself instead of staying stagnant.** (*Self-love pushes you to evolve, not stay comfortable.*)
  Loving yourself **doesn't mean staying the same**. It means respecting yourself enough to **level up**— mentally, emotionally, physically, and spiritually. Growth is an act of love, and the best thing you can do for yourself is **keep becoming the best version of you.**
- **Communicating with yourself honestly and listening to your needs.** (*Your inner voice should be your greatest ally, not your worst enemy.*) The way you talk to yourself matters. **Would you speak to a friend the way you speak to yourself?** If the answer is no, it's time to rewrite that inner dialogue. Self-love is about turning your inner voice into your **biggest supporter, not your harshest critic**.

The Difference Between Acting Like You Love Yourself vs. Actually Loving Yourself

Fake self-love is about looking the part.
Real self-love is about feeling whole within.

Fake self-love is about doing things for the 'aesthetic.'
Real self-love is about doing things because they nourish you.

Fake self-love is about proving something to others.
Real self-love is about not needing to prove anything at all.

At the end of the day, **real self-love is about treating yourself with the same love, respect, and care that you'd give to someone you truly adore**. No filters, no performance, no validation required.

So ask yourself:

Do you truly love yourself—or are you just acting like you do?

Because the deeper you go into self-love, the less you need to prove it to anyone else.

Loving Yourself for Existing—Not Just for What You Accomplish

Be honest—have you ever felt like you have to **earn** love? Like your worth is tied to **how much you do**, rather than just **who you are?**

That's how a lot of us are conditioned. We grow up thinking:

If I'm successful, I'll be valuable.

If I look good, I'll be loved.

If I make people happy, I'll be worthy.

But let's get something straight—**self-love isn't a reward.**

It's not something you unlock **after** hitting a certain level of achievement or **when** you finally feel "good enough." It's not something you get **only when** others recognize your worth.

It's something you give yourself simply because you exist.

You are not just worthy when you're productive. You are not just lovable when you look your best. You are not just valuable when others say you are.

You are enough, exactly as you are, right now. Period.

Breaking Free from Conditional Self-Worth

Think about a baby. A newborn doesn't need to accomplish **anything** to be loved. No one looks at a baby and thinks, *What have you done to deserve love today?*

They are loved just for **being**.

So why do we grow up believing we have to prove our worth?

Society trains us to think that **being enough isn't enough.** That we have to hustle, achieve, look a certain way, or meet certain expectations before we deserve love, happiness, or even rest.

But here's the truth: **Your existence is enough.**

You don't have to earn rest.

You don't have to prove your worth.

You don't have to "deserve" love—you already do.

The problem is, we've been taught that **self-worth is conditional**—that it depends on how others see us, how much we contribute, or how flawless we appear. But real, unshakable self-love comes from **knowing that you are valuable just as you are, without needing proof.**

And when you start believing that? **That's when everything changes.**

Redefining Your Worth

Start asking yourself:

Do I only feel good about myself when I'm accomplishing something?

Do I struggle to rest because I feel like I haven't "earned" it?

Do I tie my self-worth to how productive, attractive, or "useful" I am to others?

If the answer is yes, it's time to shift your mindset.

It's time to **separate your worth from your work.**

To **detach your value from other people's validation.**

To **love yourself for who you are, not just what you do.**

You are worthy on your best days.

You are worthy on your worst days.

You are worthy simply because you exist.

And once you fully embrace that? **You become unstoppable.**

Reflection Exercise: Seeing Yourself Through the Lens of Love

Find a quiet space where you won't be interrupted. Sit comfortably, take a deep breath, and close your eyes. Let go of the noise of the world for a moment—this is time for **you.**

Step 1: Imagine Yourself as a Child

Picture yourself at **five years old.** See that little version of you standing in front of you. Look at their face—the curiosity in their eyes, the innocence, the way they exist without questioning whether they deserve love.

Now, ask yourself:

Would you tell this child they have to earn love?

Would you withhold kindness from them because they haven't achieved enough?

Would you shame them for making mistakes, for not always looking perfect, for just **being human**?

Of course not. You would embrace them. You would tell them they are **worthy, loved, and enough,** just as they are.

Step 2: The Mirror of Self-Love

Now, imagine yourself standing in front of a mirror. **Really see yourself**—not just your appearance, but your essence. The person you've grown into. The person who has survived every challenge life has thrown at them. The person who has tried, failed, learned, and kept going.

Look into your own eyes and ask:

What is my current definition of self-love?

Has it been based on achievement, appearance, or what others think? Or is it rooted in deep, unconditional acceptance of myself?

How do I talk to myself on bad days?

Would I speak to a loved one the way I speak to myself when I'm struggling? If not, why do I believe I deserve less kindness than I give to others?

What's one way I can start loving myself as I am, today?

Not when I hit the next goal. **Not when I feel "better" or "prettier" or more accomplished.** Right now.

Step 3: Affirming Your Worth

Put your hand over your heart. Feel your heartbeat. **You are here. You are alive. You are enough.**

Say this out loud:

I do not have to earn my worth—it is already mine.

I release the need to prove myself to anyone, including myself.

I am allowed to rest, to grow, to be imperfect, and still be deeply worthy of love.

When you open your eyes, carry this feeling with you. Let this exercise be a reminder that **your love for yourself should never be based on conditions—it should simply be.**

Final Thoughts: Self-Love Is a Choice

Self-love isn't something you stumble into—it's something you **choose.**

Not once. Not just on good days. **Every single day.**

Because every day, you have the power to:

- **Treat yourself with kindness or criticism.** (*Will you be your biggest supporter or your harshest judge?*)
- **Trust yourself or doubt yourself.** (*Will you believe in your own wisdom or constantly second-guess yourself?*)
- **Pour into yourself or neglect yourself.** (*Will you give yourself the love you deserve, or wait for someone else to do it for you?*)

And every choice you make builds the **relationship you have with yourself.**

Think about the way you treat the people you love. You check in on them, encourage them, and want the best for them. **Do you do the same for yourself?** Or do you criticize, overwork, and abandon yourself when you need love the most?

Because self-love is more than just an idea—it's an **action.** It's in the way you:

- Talk to yourself when no one's around.
- Show up for yourself when things get hard.
- Allow yourself to rest without guilt.
- Set boundaries and stand by them.
- Choose what's best for your future, not just what feels good in the moment.

Choosing Self-Love, Even When It's Hard

Let's be real—some days, self-love doesn't feel easy. Some days, you might not feel lovable. Some days, you might fall back into old patterns of self-doubt or self-criticism.

And that's okay.

Because self-love isn't about being perfect—it's about being **committed**.

On the days when it's hard, remind yourself:

I don't have to feel perfect to be worthy.

I don't have to accomplish anything to deserve love.

I don't have to prove myself to anyone—including myself.

Self-love is the ultimate **home** you create within yourself. It's the **foundation** that holds you steady no matter what happens around you. And when you build that foundation **strong**, nothing—no failure, no rejection, no bad day—can shake it.

Your Love for Yourself Sets the Standard

So let's start making choices that **honor** who you are. Choices that reflect **self-acceptance, not self-rejection**. Choices that say:

I am worthy.

I am enough.

I am loved.

Because once you **truly** love yourself as you are—that's when life starts loving you back.

And when you choose yourself first? That's when **everything changes.**

Chapter 2: Who Am I? – Understanding Your Unique Blueprint

Let's get one thing straight—there is **no one else** on this planet like you.

No one with your exact **mind**, experiences, strengths, and perspectives.

No one with your mix of **talents, quirks, and ways of seeing the world**.

No one who can **think, feel, and create** in the way that **only you** can.

You are a **one-of-one**, completely original, **never to be duplicated**.

So why do we spend so much time trying to **fit into someone else's mold**?

Why do we measure our worth by **comparison**, trying to match an image that was never meant for us in the first place? Why do we chase definitions of success, beauty, and happiness that don't actually align with who we are?

Most people struggle with self-love because they've never taken the time to truly understand themselves.

They know how to be what **society expects**, what their **family wants**, or what **looks good on paper**—but strip all of that away, and they're left wondering:

Who am I, really?

What do I truly want, separate from what I've been told to want?

What makes me feel whole, free, and aligned?

This chapter is about **self-awareness**—the key to **customizing self-love for who you truly are**. Because self-love **isn't one-size-fits-**

all. What works for someone else may not work for you. And that's okay.

Real self-love isn't about forcing yourself to be something you're not. It's about:

Learning **who you are** beneath the expectations and labels.

Understanding **what you need** to feel safe, happy, and fulfilled.

Creating a life where you can **thrive as your most authentic self.**

Because the truth is, **you can't fully love yourself if you don't fully know yourself.**

And the more you embrace your **unique blueprint**, the more self-love starts to feel like **home**—not a struggle, not a performance, but something that comes **naturally, because it was meant just for you.**

The Power of Knowing Yourself

Self-love isn't **one-size-fits-all**. What works for one person might not work for you, and that's **okay**.

- **Some people** thrive on structure and routines—waking up at 5 AM, following a strict schedule, and planning their lives down to the minute.

- **Others** thrive on creativity and spontaneity—flowing with the moment, embracing inspiration when it strikes, and working best when they have freedom.

- **Some people** feel energized in social settings—networking, being around people, and bouncing ideas off others.

- **Others** recharge best in solitude—needing quiet time, deep thinking, and space to process their thoughts.
- **Some people** love fast-paced, high-energy environments—thriving under pressure, feeding off adrenaline, and chasing big, exciting goals.
- **Others** need peace and stability—working best in a calm space, with consistency and balance as their foundation.

And guess what? **All of these are valid.**

The problem? **We're taught to ignore our natural tendencies.**

- We're told to **"push through"** instead of respecting our limits.
- We're told that **success only looks one way**—a corporate job, a degree, a socially accepted timeline.
- We're told that **intelligence is measured by grades** instead of creativity, emotional depth, or problem-solving skills.
- We're told that **happiness comes from checking off a list of milestones**—marriage, kids, a house, a six-figure job—without ever asking if those things actually align with **us.**

And when we don't fit into that mold, we start thinking **something is wrong with us.**

But let me be clear: **Nothing is wrong with you.**

You just need to **stop forcing yourself into boxes that were never meant for you.**

The moment you stop trying to be what you *think* you should be and start honoring **who you truly are**, everything shifts.

Because when you understand **how you think, work, and function**, you stop fighting against yourself. You stop following blueprints that were designed for someone else's success and **start creating your own path.**

And the best part? **Life feels easier when you're not constantly at war with yourself.**

You don't have to change who you are—you just have to start working with yourself, not against yourself.

And that is where self-love truly begins.

Your Unique Blueprint: Understanding Your Strengths, Challenges, and Gifts

Let's break this down. **Self-awareness is about knowing three things:**

1. Your Strengths – What You Naturally Excel At

These are the things you do effortlessly, the skills that come naturally, the traits that make you unique.

Maybe you're a problem-solver. Maybe you're a deep thinker. Maybe you have an incredible way of connecting with people. Maybe your creativity is unmatched.

Whatever it is—**own it.** These are the qualities that set you apart.

Exercise: List 5 things you're naturally good at. No false humility—**own your strengths.**

2. Your Challenges – Areas for Growth

Self-love isn't just about celebrating your strengths. It's also about **accepting your flaws and working with them, not against them.**

Maybe you struggle with overthinking. Maybe you procrastinate. Maybe you have a habit of doubting yourself. **That's okay.**

The goal isn't to be perfect—it's to be **aware** of what holds you back so you can work on it *without shame.*

Exercise: List 3 personal challenges. Then, next to each one, write a small step you can take to improve it.

3. Your Needs – What Helps You Thrive

This is where most people **ignore themselves the most.** They push through environments, relationships, and habits that drain them because they think that's what they *should* do.

But real self-love is about **understanding what you need to feel your best.**

Do you need quiet time to recharge?

Do you work better in short bursts or long deep-focus sessions?

Do you feel happier when you have creative outlets?

Do you need structure, or does routine make you feel trapped?

When you **respect your needs instead of ignoring them**, life flows *so* much easier.

Exercise: What are 3 things you need to feel happy, energized, and focused?

Breaking Bad Mental Habits & Forming New Ones

Understanding yourself is **step one. Step two?** Breaking the habits that keep you **stuck.**

Because self-awareness means nothing if you keep running the same mental loops that hold you back. And the truth is, **a lot of us have mental habits we don't even realize are limiting us.**

Let's talk about them.

Mental Habits That Keep You Stuck:
Negative Self-Talk:
"I'm not good at this."

"I always mess up."

"I'll never be successful."

Your words create your reality. If you keep speaking against yourself, don't be surprised when your life reflects that.

Self-Sabotage:
Avoiding opportunities out of fear of failure.

Procrastinating on things that actually matter to you.

Doubting yourself to the point of inaction.

Sometimes, we're so afraid of failing that we don't even try—so we **fail by default.**

People-Pleasing:
Saying yes when you really mean no.

Worrying about what others think more than what you want.

Feeling guilty for prioritizing yourself.

You can't build a life you love if you're constantly living for **everyone else**.

Comparing Yourself:

Feeling like you're "behind" because of what others are achieving.

Scrolling through social media and doubting your own progress.

Measuring your worth based on someone else's timeline.

Comparison **steals your joy** and blinds you to your own **growth and uniqueness**.

The Good News? You Can Rewire Your Brain.

Your mind is like an **operating system**. And just like a phone or computer, it can be **updated, upgraded, and reprogrammed**.

Here's how to replace those **toxic thought loops** with new mental habits that actually support you:

Reframing Self-Talk:
- Instead of *"I always mess up,"* → say *"I'm still learning, and that's okay."*
- Instead of *"I'm not good at this,"* → say *"I'm improving every time I try."*
- Instead of *"I'll never succeed,"* → say *"Success is built on growth, and I'm growing."*

Your words are **powerful**, so choose ones that build you up instead of tearing you down.

Taking Small Risks:
Instead of **avoiding things out of fear**, take small steps outside your comfort zone.
- Apply for the opportunity, even if you don't feel "ready."
- Speak up for yourself, even if it feels uncomfortable.

- Try something new, even if you're scared of failing.

Confidence doesn't come **before** action—it comes **from** action.

Setting Boundaries:

Instead of **saying yes to everything**, pause and ask yourself:

"Do I actually want to do this?"

"Does this align with what I need right now?"

The more you respect your own time and energy, the more others will too.

Focusing on Your Own Path:

Instead of **comparing yourself**, remind yourself:

"Their journey is theirs. Mine is mine."

"I'm not behind—I'm on my own timeline."

"No one else has my exact path, and that's my power."

The only person you should compare yourself to is **who you were yesterday**.

Exercise: Reset Your Mental Patterns

Pick **ONE** bad mental habit you want to break. Write it down.

Now, write down what you'll replace it with. Every time that habit creeps up, use your **new thought pattern** to override it.

Example:

Old Habit: *"I'm not good enough."*

New Habit: *"I am growing, evolving, and worthy exactly as I am."*

The more you repeat the **new belief**, the faster your mind rewires itself to support the person you're becoming.

Because when you **upgrade your mindset**, your whole life **levels up**.

Loving the Way You Think, Work, and Create

Self-love isn't just about **who you are**—it's also about **how you operate**.

Some people are **deep thinkers** who love analyzing everything. They need time to process, reflect, and explore all possibilities before making a decision.

Some are **action-takers** who learn best by doing. They thrive on movement, experience, and hands-on learning, figuring things out as they go.

Some people are **planners** who thrive on organization, structure, and having a clear roadmap. They feel best when they know what's coming next and can prepare for it.

Some are **free spirits** who need flexibility, spontaneity, and creative flow. They feel trapped by rigid schedules and do their best work when they have freedom.

And guess what? **All of these are valid.**

There is no "right" way to think.

There is no "best" way to work.

There is no single way to create or be productive.

There's only **what works for you.**

If You Struggle with Feeling "Different" from Others, Ask Yourself:

- *Am I really flawed, or do I just have a different way of thinking?*

(Maybe school, work, or society made me feel like my way was "wrong," but what if it's actually a strength?)

- *Have I been trying to force myself into a way of working that doesn't fit me?*

(Am I pushing myself to be something I'm not instead of embracing how I naturally function?)

- *How can I start embracing my natural strengths instead of resisting them?*

(What if I stopped trying to "fix" the way I think and instead leaned into it as my superpower?)

The Shift That Changes Everything

When you stop trying to **work against yourself** and start **working with yourself**, everything gets easier.

You stop forcing yourself into systems that **don't match your energy**.

You stop feeling like you need to **"keep up" with others** and instead **own your own rhythm**.

You stop judging yourself for being "different" and start realizing that your way of thinking, working, and creating is **what makes you powerful.**

The way your mind works is not a mistake. It's your blueprint, your advantage, and your gift.

So instead of trying to fit into someone else's mold—**break it.**

And start loving yourself for the way you **think, work, and create.**

Final Thoughts: You Are Not Supposed to Be Like Everyone Else

The sooner you accept that **your path is your own**, the sooner you'll stop feeling like you're **falling behind**.

Because the truth is—**you were never meant to follow someone else's timeline.**

You don't have to learn like everyone else.

(*Your mind works in a way that's unique to you—lean into that, not against it.*)

You don't have to succeed like everyone else.

(*Your version of success doesn't have to look like anyone else's. Define it for yourself.*)

You don't have to fit into anyone's definition of what's normal.

(*Normal is a social construct anyway—why blend in when you were made to stand out?*)

You just have to:

Understand yourself. (*Know how you think, learn, and thrive.*)

Love yourself. (*Honor your strengths, work with your challenges, and embrace your uniqueness.*)

Move accordingly. (*Live life on your own terms, not based on someone else's rulebook.*)

Because **you were built differently on purpose.**

And the moment you stop **shrinking to fit in**, stop **comparing your timeline**, stop **thinking you're behind**— is the moment you finally start **thriving**. Own who you are. **That's where your power is.**

Chapter 3: Loving Your Mind, Body, and Soul

Self-love isn't just about how you **feel** about yourself—it's about how you **treat** yourself.

And that means honoring **every part of you**: your **mind**, your **body**, and your **soul**.

Too many people struggle with self-love because they're **constantly at war with themselves.**

They wish their **personality** was different.

They **criticize** their flaws instead of understanding them.

They **ignore their intuition** because they've been conditioned to doubt themselves.

They **push their needs aside** just to fit into society's expectations.

But **real self-love?** It's not about perfection. It's about **radical acceptance**.

Not just loving the **"good"** parts of yourself, but embracing **the whole package**—flaws, quirks, strengths, and all.

Because when you spend your life **fighting against yourself**, you stay stuck. But when you learn to **work with yourself**, you grow, heal, and thrive.

This chapter is about learning how to be **on your own team.** How to **work with yourself instead of against yourself.** How to **listen to what you need**, instead of chasing what the world tells you to be.

Because **self-love isn't just a feeling—it's a daily choice.**

So let's get into it.

1. How to Genuinely Accept Your Personality, Flaws, and Strengths

Flaws Are Not Failures—They're Just Parts of You

Let's be real: **We all have things about ourselves we wish we could change.**

We've been taught to see certain traits as "bad," to feel like we need to "fix" ourselves to be worthy. But **self-love doesn't mean pretending your flaws don't exist—it means accepting them without shame.**

Because the truth is, **your 'flaws' are often just perspectives.** What one person sees as a weakness, another sees as a strength.

- **Too sensitive?** No—you're emotionally intelligent and deeply connected to your feelings.
- **Overthinker?** No—you analyze deeply and see details others miss.
- **Too quiet?** No—you observe, listen, and process things differently.
- **Impatient?** No—you know what you want and don't waste time.
- **Too independent?** No—you're self-sufficient and don't need external validation.

How you **see** yourself matters. Because if you keep labeling parts of yourself as "bad," you'll keep **rejecting pieces of who you are.**

But imagine what would happen if you **embraced those parts instead.**

What if instead of trying to "fix" yourself, you worked on **understanding yourself?**

What if instead of seeing flaws as something to erase, you saw them as part of your unique **blueprint**?

What if instead of wishing you were different, you realized you were **designed this way for a reason**?

Your **flaws** don't make you **less** worthy of love. Your **imperfections** don't make you **unworthy** of happiness. Your **uniqueness** is not a **problem to be solved—it's a gift to be embraced.**

Exercise: Write down **one thing** you've always seen as a flaw. Now, **reframe it**—how could this actually be a **strength**?

Your Strengths Deserve More Love

Why is it so **easy** to focus on what's "wrong" with us, but so **hard** to acknowledge what's *right*?

Think about it:

You've overcome things that would've broken others.

You've learned, grown, and adapted in ways you don't even realize.

You have talents, qualities, and experiences that make you irreplaceable.

But how often do you **stop and acknowledge** those things?

Self-love isn't just about **accepting your flaws**—it's about **celebrating your strengths.**

Maybe you're **resilient**—you've been through challenges and came out stronger.

Maybe you're **creative**—you have a way of seeing the world that others don't.

Maybe you're **loyal**—you love deeply and protect the people you care about.

Maybe you're **driven**—when you want something, you go after it with full force.

Maybe you're **funny, resourceful, intuitive, adaptable, or wise.**

It's time to start **giving yourself credit.**

Exercise: List **three things** you genuinely **love** about yourself. No downplaying, no false humility. Just **own it.**

Because **the way you see yourself sets the standard for how the world sees you.**

And once you start treating yourself like you're **worthy, enough, and powerful**—that's exactly what you become.

2. Your Mind's Algorithm – How Your Thoughts Create Your Reality

Your brain is like an **algorithm**—it reinforces **whatever you focus on the most.**

Think about it like a social media feed. When you constantly engage with certain content, the algorithm starts showing you **more of the same.** Your mind works the same way.

If you constantly think:

I'm not good enough.

I always mess up.

I'm never going to succeed.

Your brain will start scanning your life for **proof** that these statements are true. It will highlight your failures, remind you of past mistakes, and make sure you stay stuck in that belief.

But if you start thinking:

✔ *I am capable.*

✔ *I am learning.*

✔ *I am becoming better every day.*

Your brain will start filtering **for that reality instead.**

This is not **toxic positivity**—it's **science.** Your **thoughts shape your beliefs, your beliefs shape your actions, and your actions shape your reality.**

Rewiring Your Mental Algorithm

To break free from negative thought loops, you have to start **feeding your mind new evidence.**

Negative Thought: *"I'm not good at anything."*

Reframe: *"I haven't found my strengths yet, but I'm learning more about myself every day."*

Negative Thought: *"I always mess things up."*

Reframe: *"I make mistakes like everyone else, but I grow from them."*

Negative Thought: *"Nothing ever works out for me."*

Reframe: *"Challenges are temporary. I am resilient, and I figure things out."*

Your Inner Dialogue is Everything

The way you **speak to yourself** is just as important as the way you **treat yourself.**

Would you tell a child they're **a failure** for making mistakes?

Would you tell a friend they're **not good enough** when they're struggling?

No? Then **why do you say those things to yourself?**

You are **not your worst thoughts.** You are **not your past mistakes.**

You are **who you choose to believe you are.**

Exercise: Rewire Your Thoughts

1. **Write down one negative thought** you catch yourself repeating.
2. **Reframe it into a truth** that supports you instead of tearing you down.
3. **Repeat it to yourself daily**—especially when the old thought tries to creep in.

Because when you start **training your mind to work for you instead of against you,** everything starts to change.

Your thoughts create your reality. **Choose them wisely.**

3. The Power of Your Gut Feeling and Intuition

You always know.

Even when you **doubt yourself.**

Even when you **ignore it.**

Even when you try to **convince yourself otherwise**—your **gut knows.**

So why don't we listen?

Most of us have been **conditioned** to doubt our own instincts.

- We **overthink** instead of trusting our first instinct.
- We **seek external validation**, waiting for others to confirm what we already feel.
- We **rationalize red flags**, convincing ourselves we're just being dramatic.

But **self-love means trusting yourself.**

Trusting that your feelings are **valid.**

Trusting that your intuition is **guiding you toward what's meant for you.**

Trusting that your inner voice **knows what's best for you—even when logic, people, or fear tell you otherwise.**

You've Felt It Before

Ever gotten a weird vibe about someone but ignored it—then later realized you were right?

Ever had a gut feeling about a decision, but second-guessed yourself and regretted it?

Ever felt drawn to something without knowing why, and it ended up being exactly what you needed?

That's **your intuition** trying to protect you. And the more you **listen to it**, the **stronger it gets.**

Ignoring your intuition is like ignoring a personal guide that's **always looking out for you.** The problem is, we're so used to **dismissing it** that we don't even recognize it anymore.

But the good news? **You can rebuild that connection.**

How to Strengthen Your Intuition

Practice stillness.

Your intuition can't get through if your mind is always cluttered. Meditation, journaling, nature walks, or even just sitting in silence can help you hear yourself again.

Notice patterns.

Look back at times your gut was **right**—even when you didn't listen. The more you recognize this, the more trust you'll build in yourself.

Check in with your body.

Your intuition often **speaks through physical sensations**—tightness, ease, excitement, dread. If something **feels off**, don't ignore it. Your body is always giving you clues.

Stop seeking outside opinions for everything.

Next time you have a decision to make, pause. **Ask yourself first**—before you ask anyone else. The more you trust yourself, the less you'll need constant reassurance.

Exercise: Strengthen Your Intuition

1. **Think of a time your intuition was right.**
- How did it feel? What signals did your body give you?
2. **Think of a time you ignored it.**
- What happened as a result? What did you learn from that experience?
3. **How can you start trusting that feeling more moving forward?**
- Write down one way you'll honor your intuition the next time it speaks to you.

4. Listening to Your Needs, Not Society's Expectations

Let's be real—**society will always try to tell you who you should be.**

- **You should work non-stop** to be successful. (*Because hustle culture says rest is for the weak.*)
- **You should look a certain way** to be attractive. (*As if beauty is one-size-fits-all.*)
- **You should be in a relationship** by a certain age. (*As if your worth depends on your relationship status.*)

But here's the truth: **None of these expectations matter if they don't align with your truth.**

You weren't put on this earth to follow a **pre-written script**.

You don't have to **chase things you don't actually want** just because society tells you to.

You don't have to **measure your success, happiness, or self-worth** by what the world says is "right."

Real self-love means **listening to yourself more than you listen to external noise.**

How to Start Listening to What You Need

Check in with yourself daily.

Ask: *What do I need today?* More rest? More focus? More boundaries? The more you tune into yourself, the easier it gets to honor your needs.

Question everything.

If you're chasing a goal, pause and ask: *Do I actually want this, or was I told I should want this?* If the answer is **unclear**, sit with it. Your desires should feel like yours, not something borrowed.

Honor your unique path.

Just because something works for **others** doesn't mean it's right for **you**. Your life doesn't have to look like anyone else's. In fact, it **shouldn't**—because you are not them.

Set boundaries against expectations that don't serve you. You don't owe the world a version of yourself that isn't real. The more you **say no to what drains you, the more space you create for what actually fulfills you.**

Exercise: Break Free from Societal Pressure

1. **Write down one societal expectation you've felt pressured by.**

(*Example: "I should have a traditional 9-to-5 job to be successful."*)

2. **Now, ask yourself:**

- *Is this something I actually want, or have I been conditioned to think I should want it?*
- *Does this goal align with who I truly am, or am I chasing it to prove something to others?*

3. **Decide what's true for YOU.**

If it aligns with your **real desires,** embrace it. If it doesn't, **release it**—you are allowed to build a life that actually makes sense for YOU.

Because when you start **listening to yourself instead of society**, that's when you truly start **living.**

Final Thoughts: Self-Love Means Honoring All of You

Loving yourself isn't just about **saying nice things to yourself—**it's about **how you show up for yourself every day.**

It's about:

Accepting every part of who you are—flaws, strengths, quirks, and all. (*No more picking and choosing which parts of yourself deserve love—you deserve it all.*)

Reprogramming your mind to work for you, not against you. (*Because your thoughts shape your reality, and you deserve a mindset that uplifts you.*)

Trusting your own instincts instead of doubting yourself. (*You already have the answers—you just have to start listening.*)

Rejecting expectations that don't align with your truth. (*You are not here to follow someone else's script—you are here to write your own.*)

Because **self-love isn't just about feeling good**—it's about **knowing yourself, trusting yourself, and honoring yourself in every way possible.**

And when you do that?

You become unstoppable.

Chapter 4: The Power of Your Words – Speaking Love Into Yourself

Let's get one thing straight—**your words are spells.**

Every word you speak, every thought you repeat, every phrase you casually throw out—**it's all shaping your reality.**

Whether you realize it or not, you are **constantly programming your mind.**

If you tell yourself:

I'm not good enough.

I always mess up.

I'll never be successful.

Your brain **believes it.** It scans your life for **proof**, reinforcing the belief and making sure you stay stuck.

But when you affirm:

I am capable.

I am learning.

I deserve good things.

Your brain **starts adjusting to that truth**, shifting your actions, energy, and mindset to align with it.

Because the way you **speak to yourself** is either **building you up or tearing you down. There is no in-between.**

So if you've been waiting for a sign to start talking to yourself with **love, confidence, and power—**

This is it.

1. Every Word You Speak Plants a Seed

Think of your mind like a **garden**. Every **word you speak**, every **thought you repeat**, is a **seed**.

Negative words plant **weeds**—they spread, take over, and suffocate your growth.

Positive words plant **flowers**—they bloom, flourish, and create beauty in your life.

Now, ask yourself: **What are you planting?**

If you constantly say:

I'm not smart enough.

I'll never find love.

I'm bad at everything.

Then guess what? **Those thoughts take root.** They become the foundation of your **self-image, your energy, and your actions.** They grow into your reality, shaping how you **see yourself and how you move through life.**

Your mind doesn't argue—it simply **accepts what you repeatedly tell it.**

Words Have Power—Use Them Wisely

The good news? **You can change what you plant.**

Start speaking to yourself with **the same love and encouragement you'd give to a close friend.** Instead of reinforcing negativity, choose words that **empower and uplift you.**

If you start saying:

I am always learning and improving. (Growth is my natural state.)

I attract love effortlessly. (I am surrounded by love in all forms.)

I have strengths that make me valuable. (I bring something unique to every space I enter.)

Then **those** beliefs take root instead. They start growing. They start shaping the way you **see yourself, the energy you carry, and the opportunities you attract.**

Because the **words you repeat daily** become your **truth.**

Your Words Shape Your Self-Worth

Imagine two people.

Person A wakes up and says:

"I hate the way I look. I'm so lazy. Nothing good ever happens to me."

They carry **low energy, self-doubt, and frustration** throughout the day. They shrink, hesitate, and reinforce their belief that they're not enough.

Person B wakes up and says:

"I am learning to love myself more every day. I am capable and worthy of success. I attract the right people and opportunities."

They carry **confidence, openness, and resilience** throughout the day. They walk with purpose, take action, and attract situations that reinforce their self-worth.

The **difference?** Their words. **Same world, different reality.**

Which one do you want to be?

Exercise: Rewriting Your Script

1. **Write down one negative phrase** you catch yourself saying often. (*Be honest—what's that one thought you default to when you're feeling low?*)

2. **Now, rewrite it into a positive, empowering statement.**

- Instead of *"I'm not good enough,"* → say *"I am always growing, evolving, and improving."*
- Instead of *"I always mess things up,"* → say *"I learn from every experience and get better each time."*

3. **Repeat it daily.** Put it on your mirror, in your phone, or say it out loud every morning.

Because when you **speak to yourself with love, confidence, and power**, you start to **become** that person.

And **that's how you rewrite your reality.**

2. How Positive Affirmations Rewire Your Mindset

Affirmations aren't just **cute phrases**—they're **brain training**.

Every time you **repeat a positive statement**, your brain forms **new neural pathways** that support that belief. The more you repeat it, the stronger those pathways become.

Think of it like working out.

You don't see results after one session—but over time, **your muscles grow stronger, your endurance builds, and your body adapts.**

Your **mind** works the same way.

At first, saying positive affirmations might feel awkward or fake—especially if you're used to negative self-talk. But just like **lifting weights**, the more you do it, the **stronger the belief becomes.**

Until one day, you realize... you don't just **say** the affirmation anymore—**you believe it.**

How Affirmations Work in Real Life

Your mind is **always listening,** and it doesn't know the difference between **a fact and a repeated belief.**

If you constantly think:

I'm not good enough.

I'll never be confident.

Nothing ever works out for me.

Your brain **accepts those statements as truth** and filters your experiences to match them.

But if you replace those thoughts with:

I am worthy, just as I am.

I carry confidence in everything I do.

Opportunities flow to me with ease.

Your mind **adjusts to that reality instead.**

Your **thoughts** shift → Your **beliefs** shift → Your **actions** shift → Your **life** shifts.

How to Make Affirmations Work for You

Say them in the present tense.

- *I am confident.* (*Not: I will be confident*)
- *I am deserving of love.* (*Not: One day, I'll be loved*)

Your brain responds best to what's **happening now**—not what might happen "someday."

Make them personal.

- *I trust myself completely.* (*Not just: People trust me.*)

- *I am enough as I am.* (*Not: Everyone else is enough, so maybe I am too.*)

Your affirmations should **speak directly to YOU**—they are for **your** growth and transformation.

Repeat them daily.
- Say them in the mirror. (*Look yourself in the eye and own it.*)
- Write them down. (*Seeing them reinforces the message in your mind.*)
- Say them before bed. (*Your subconscious absorbs what you tell it right before sleep.*)

Feel them.
- Don't just say the words—**believe them.**
- Speak them with **conviction, emotion, and power.**
- Imagine what it **feels like** for them to already be true.

Because the **words you say with belief** will **reprogram your mind faster than anything else.**

Exercise: Create Your Power Affirmation
   1. Think of one negative belief you've been holding onto.
   (*Example: "I'm not confident."*)
   2. Rewrite it into a powerful affirmation in the present tense.
   (*Example: "I radiate confidence in everything I do."*)
   3. Say it out loud, right now.

4. Commit to repeating it daily—morning, night, whenever doubt creeps in.

Because the more you **say it**, the more you **believe it**—and once you believe it? **You become it.**

3. How to Stop Negative Self-Talk in Its Tracks

Catching negative self-talk is the first step. Because most of the time, we don't even realize we're doing it.

Our minds run on **autopilot**, repeating thoughts we've been conditioned to believe—many of which **aren't even true.**

But here's the thing: **You are not your thoughts. You are the observer of your thoughts.**

And that means you have the power to **change them.**

Here's How to Break the Cycle:

Step 1: Notice the Thought

The first step is **awareness**. Pay attention to the way you speak to yourself, especially in moments of frustration or doubt.

"I'm so bad at this."

"I always make mistakes."

"I'm never going to be successful."

Would you let someone else talk to you like this? **Then why do you allow it from yourself?**

Step 2: Question It

Is this actually true? (*Or is this just fear talking?*)

Would I say this to someone I love? (*If not, why do I say it to myself?*)

Is there evidence that proves otherwise? (*Have I succeeded before? Have I learned from mistakes before?*)

Negative self-talk thrives when it goes **unquestioned.** But when you **challenge it,** you start to see it for what it really is—**a lie your mind made up.**

Step 3: Replace It with Truth

Once you recognize that the negative thought **isn't serving you,** you can replace it with **one that does.**

"I'm so bad at this." - *"I'm still learning, and I'm getting better every day."*

"I always make mistakes." - *"Mistakes help me grow—I learn from them and move forward."*

"I'm never going to be successful." - *"Success is a process, and every step I take is bringing me closer."*

At first, it might feel fake. That's normal—because your brain is **used to negativity.**

But the more you **reframe your thoughts**, the more your mind starts believing the new reality you're creating.

The Goal: Progress, Not Perfection

The goal isn't to **never have negative thoughts**—that's impossible.

The goal is to **catch them, question them, and replace them with something empowering** before they take root.

Negative thoughts are like **intrusive ads on your mental feed—**you don't have to engage with them. **You can scroll past and choose better.**

Exercise: Reframe Your Thoughts in Real Time

1. Catch one negative thought today. (*Be honest with yourself—what do you tend to tell yourself when things don't go right?*)

2. Write it down. (*Seeing it on paper takes away its power.*)

3. Reframe it into something empowering. (*What's a truth that actually serves you?*)

Because the more you **replace self-doubt with self-support,** the stronger and more unstoppable you become.

4. Speak to Yourself Like Someone You Love

If your **best friend** was struggling, would you ever look them in the eye and say:

"Wow, you're such a failure."

"You'll never be good enough."

"No one cares about you."

Of course not. **So why do you talk to yourself that way?**

We are often **our own worst critics,** saying things to ourselves that we would **never** say to someone we care about.

But here's the truth:

You deserve the same love, encouragement, and kindness that you give to others.

Think about how **gentle, supportive, and patient** you are when a friend is hurting. Now ask yourself:

What if I spoke to myself with that same love?

What if I became my own biggest supporter instead of my harshest critic?

The Rule: If You Wouldn't Say It to Someone You Love, Don't Say It to Yourself. Period.

Next time you catch yourself being cruel to yourself, pause and ask:

Would I say this to my best friend?

Would I say this to a child who was struggling?

Would I say this to someone I deeply love and respect?

If the answer is **no**, then it has **no place in your self-talk.**

Because **you** deserve that same level of love, patience, and grace.

Start treating yourself like someone **worth protecting, worth uplifting, and worth believing in**—because you **are.**

5. Daily Affirmation Practice: Rewiring Your Mindset

If you're ready to start **speaking love into yourself**, it's time to make affirmations a **daily habit.**

Affirmations aren't just words—they are **instructions for your mind.**

The more you **repeat them**, the more your brain rewires itself to believe them. And the more you **believe them**, the more your actions, energy, and confidence **align with them.**

Daily Affirmations to Speak Over Yourself

"I am worthy. I am enough. I am loved."

"I trust myself. I believe in my own power."

"My words create my reality, and I choose to speak positivity."

"I am growing, evolving, and becoming the best version of myself."

"Every challenge is shaping me into someone stronger."

"I deserve love, success, and happiness—just as I am."

How to Make Affirmations Work for You

Choose the ones that resonate with you. (*Affirmations should feel personal and meaningful to you.*)

Say them out loud every day. (*Morning, before bed, or anytime you need a boost.*)

Look yourself in the mirror as you say them. (*This strengthens self-connection and confidence.*)

Write them down. (*Journaling affirmations helps reinforce them in your subconscious.*)

Feel them. (*Don't just say the words—let them sink in and truly believe them.*)

Your Words Are Magic—Use Them Wisely

The more you **repeat these affirmations**, the more they become **your truth**.

Because when you **speak love into yourself**, the world responds accordingly.

Final Thoughts: Your Words Are Your Superpower

Every word you speak is shaping your reality.

So start using them **with intention.** Speak to yourself **with love, with power, with confidence.**

Because when you change the way you talk to yourself, you change the way you see yourself. And when you change the way you see yourself—**you change your entire life.**

Affirmation Reminder: "I am worthy. I am enough. I am loved."
Say it. Believe it. Live it.

Chapter 5: Main Character Energy – Owning Your Worth

Let's get one thing straight—**you are not a supporting character in your own life.**

You were **never meant** to sit on the sidelines, **dim your light**, or **wait for permission** to take up space.

You were born to be **center stage**, to move through life with **confidence**, and to embrace your **power without apology.**

That's **main character energy.**

And no, it's **not** about arrogance. It's **not** about being flashy. It's **not** about proving anything to anyone.

It's about owning your worth.

It's about trusting yourself.

It's about living with purpose and moving like you belong—because you do.

So if you've been **playing small**, if you've been **waiting for external validation**, if you've been treating yourself like an **extra in someone else's movie—**

It's time to rewrite the script.

Because the moment you step into your **power**, the moment you stop **asking for permission to be great—**

Everything in your life shifts.

1. How to Stop Playing the Side Character in Your Own Life

Are you the **star of your own story**, or are you just **watching it unfold** from the background?

Too many people live their lives **like a side character**—waiting, hesitating, letting the world decide their fate. But here's the thing: **this is YOUR life. YOUR movie. YOUR story.**

A side character:
Waits for things to happen instead of **making** things happen.
Lets other people dictate their choices.
Settles for whatever comes their way instead of **going after what they want.**
Downplays their worth, thinking they don't deserve more.
Seeks approval before making decisions, afraid to disappoint others.

A main character:
Takes charge of their own story—because no one else can.
Chooses what aligns with their goals, values, and vision.
Moves through life with purpose, confidence, and clarity.
Embraces their uniqueness, knowing that they bring something special to the world.
Doesn't wait for permission—they step forward and claim what's theirs.

Are You Living Like the Main Character in Your Own Life?

Ask yourself:
Do I actively create my life, or do I just react to what happens?

Do I make decisions based on what I truly want, or based on what others expect of me?

Am I pursuing the things that set my soul on fire, or am I playing it safe?

Because here's the truth—**no one is coming to hand you the life you want.**

If you've been:

- **Putting yourself last, always prioritizing others over your own needs**
- **Letting fear control your decisions, waiting for the "right" moment.**
- **Hiding your true self, playing small to avoid judgment**
- **Letting other people's opinions dictate your path**

Then **it's time to step into the spotlight.**

You do **not** need validation.

You do **not** need to shrink yourself to make others comfortable.

You do **not** need to wait for someone else to choose you.

You choose YOU.

You were **always meant to be the main character**—the one who takes risks, follows their dreams, and creates a life they actually love.

No more waiting. No more shrinking. No more background role.

Your story starts now. Own it.

2. Confidence vs. Cockiness – Embodying Self-Assurance Without Ego

There's a **huge** difference between **confidence and cockiness**—and if you want to **embody main character energy**, it's important to know where that line is.

Because confidence? **That's magnetic. That's power. That's the energy that makes people gravitate toward you.**

Cockiness? **That's insecurity in disguise.** It's a performance, a mask, a desperate need to be seen as important.

Confidence vs. Cockiness—What's the Difference?

Confidence is knowing your worth.

Cockiness is trying to prove it.

Confidence is quiet—it doesn't need validation.

Cockiness is loud—it's always seeking approval.

A **confident person** moves **like they belong** without needing to convince anyone.

A **cocky person** is constantly **trying to prove they belong**—usually by tearing others down.

Confident Energy Looks Like:

Knows they belong without needing to prove it. (*They don't have to announce their worth—they just move like they know it.*)

Compliments others without feeling threatened. (*Because secure people don't see others as competition.*)

Takes up space unapologetically but respects others' space too. (*Confidence is strong but never overbearing.*)

Walks into a room knowing they are valuable—even if no one acknowledges it. (*Because their worth isn't tied to external validation.*)

Cocky Energy Looks Like:

Feels the need to be the loudest in the room. (*Cocky people overcompensate for insecurity by demanding attention.*)

Puts others down to feel better about themselves. (*True confidence never requires making others feel small.*)

Needs constant validation to feel secure. (*If external approval disappears, their self-worth crumbles.*)

The Goal? Embodying Confident Energy Without Ego

Confidence isn't about being **better than anyone else**—it's about knowing **you're already enough.**

It's about:

Moving with self-assurance, even when no one is watching.

Trusting yourself, even when others doubt you.

Knowing your worth, even when the world doesn't validate it.

A confident person doesn't walk into a room and think:

"I'm better than everyone here."

They walk in and think:

"I belong here just as much as anyone else."

Exercise: Embodying Main Character Confidence

1. Think of someone whose confidence you admire. (*It could be a public figure, a friend, or even a fictional character.*)

2. Ask yourself: *What do they do differently? How do they carry themselves? How do they respond to challenges?*

3. Write down one way you can embody that same energy in your own life.

Because confidence isn't something you wait for—it's something you **step into.**

3. Why Self-Love Is the Key to Main Character Energy

Main character energy isn't just about **how you show up**—it's about **how you feel about yourself** when no one's watching.

And at the root of it all? **Self-love.**

Because when you **truly love yourself**:

You stop tolerating things that don't align with your worth. (*No more settling for less—whether it's in relationships, work, or the way you're treated.*)

You stop looking for outside validation to feel good about yourself. (*You already know your value—you don't need anyone else to confirm it.*)

You start moving through life with a natural confidence that doesn't waver. (*Not because you have it all figured out, but because you trust yourself no matter what.*)

Where Most People Go Wrong

Most people **look for confidence in external things**:

Looks (*Thinking confidence comes from how attractive they are.*)

Achievements (*Thinking self-worth is tied to success or accolades.*)

Social status (*Thinking their value is based on popularity, attention, or approval from others.*)

But real confidence? **It doesn't come from any of that.**

Real confidence comes from knowing that even without all of those things, you are still worthy.

It's about walking into any situation and knowing you belong—not because of what you have, but because of who you are.

The Self-Love Shift: Becoming Unshakable

When you build your confidence on **external things**, it's fragile. **One bad day, one mistake, one rejection—and suddenly, it's gone.**

But when your confidence is built on **self-love**, it's **unshakable**.

Because even if:

Your looks change...

Your job title shifts...

People don't validate you the way you want...

You still know: **I am enough. Just as I am.**

And **that's** what gives you true **main character energy**.

4. How to Stop Seeking Validation and Be Unapologetically Yourself

The **biggest thing** that holds people back from their **main character era**?

Caring too much about what other people think.

Let's be real—how many times have you:

Hesitated to do something you wanted because you were afraid of judgment?

Dimmed your personality to fit in or avoid standing out?

Held back from expressing yourself because you worried about what people would say?

But here's the truth:

No matter what you do, people will always have opinions. (*You could be the ripest, juiciest peach, and someone will still hate peaches.*)

Someone will always misunderstand you. (*People see you through their own lens—it has nothing to do with you.*)

Someone will always judge you. (*Even if you play it safe, even if you try to please everyone—it's impossible.*)

So **why waste time living for their approval?**

Because the moment you stop seeking validation and **start doing what actually makes you happy—you take back your power.**

How to Stop Living for Other People's Approval

Do things that make YOU feel good.

- Stop asking, *"Will people like this?"*
- Start asking, *"Do I like this?"*

Say what you mean.

- Stop **watering yourself down** to make others comfortable.
- Your **voice, your opinions, and your truth matter.**

Stop explaining yourself.

- You don't owe anyone an explanation for your **choices, boundaries, or goals.**
- If it feels right for you, **that's all that matters.**

Make peace with being misunderstood.

- **Not everyone will get you—and that's okay.**

- You are **not here to be liked by everyone**—you are here to be **yourself.**

Wear what you want, post what you want, do what makes you happy.

- The **most magnetic people** are the ones who live **unapologetically.**
- When you stop chasing approval, you start attracting people who love you for **who you really are.**

The Ultimate Mindset Shift

If you **live for their approval, you'll die by their rejection.**

But if you **validate yourself first,** no one's opinion can shake you.

So choose yourself. Every time.

Final Thoughts: It's Time to Take Up Space

Main character energy isn't about **being better than anyone else.**

It's about recognizing that **you are just as deserving as anyone else.**

You deserve to be heard. (*Your voice matters—use it.*)

You deserve to take up space. (*You don't need to shrink to make others comfortable.*)

You deserve to live a life that makes YOU happy. (*Not one that just looks good to others.*)

Because the moment you start **showing up for yourself,** unapologetically and fully—**you become unstoppable.**

No more playing small.

No more waiting for permission.
It's your story. It's your time. Own it.

Affirmation: *"I am the main character in my own life. I take up space. I own my worth. I live unapologetically."*

Say it. Believe it. **Be it.**

Part 2: How Self-Love Transforms Your Life

Loving yourself isn't just about feeling good—it's about **changing the way you move through the world.**

Because when you love yourself, **everything shifts.**

Your mindset changes. You stop doubting yourself and start believing in your power.

Your relationships change. You stop tolerating toxic energy and start surrounding yourself with people who genuinely support you.

Your decisions change. You stop settling and start choosing what actually aligns with your worth.

Self-love isn't just an inner feeling—it's an outer transformation. It affects how you approach challenges, how you handle setbacks, how you walk into a room, and how you navigate the highs and lows of life.

This section is about **applying self-love in real life.**

We're covering:

How self-love changes the way you approach your goals, challenges, and failures.

The truth about motivation—it's not about forcing yourself, it's about understanding yourself.

How to build relationships that uplift you instead of drain you.

How protecting your energy, setting boundaries, and keeping things private can be a form of self-respect.

Self-love isn't just about feeling good **when things are easy**—it's about knowing your worth **when life tests you.** It's about walking through the world with a different kind of energy—the kind that says:

I know who I am. I know what I deserve. And I refuse to settle for less.

Let's get into it.

Chapter 6: Applying Self-Love to Your Daily Life

Self-love isn't just a **feeling**—it's an **action**.

It's a **daily practice** that shapes:

How you move through life. (*Do you walk with confidence or hesitation?*)

How you handle challenges. (*Do you show yourself grace or self-criticism?*)

How you go after what you want. (*Do you believe in yourself or doubt yourself before you even begin?*)

A lot of people think **self-love is easy**—that it's just about saying nice things to yourself, taking bubble baths, or "choosing happiness."

But **real self-love?** That's how you show up for yourself when things get **hard**.

It's how you push through setbacks without self-destruction. (*Not punishing yourself for mistakes, but learning from them.*)

It's how you stay committed to your growth without burnout. (*Not forcing progress, but finding balance.*)

It's how you chase your goals with passion—not pressure. (*Not proving your worth, but aligning with it.*)

Because when you **truly** love yourself:

You don't just **work hard**—you **work smart**.

You don't just **force success**—you **align with it**.

And most importantly? You find a **balance** that actually **works for you**.

This chapter is all about **making self-love a part of your daily life**—in a way that's real, sustainable, and powerful.

1. How Self-Love Changes the Way You Approach Goals, Challenges, and Failure

Your **relationship with yourself** determines how you approach **everything**—your goals, your setbacks, and even your successes.

The way you **treat yourself** in these moments sets the tone for your entire life.

With Self-Love:

- **You pursue goals because you genuinely want them**— not because you're trying to prove something. (*You move with passion, not pressure.*)
- **You bounce back from failure** because you don't take it as a personal attack on your worth. (*A mistake is just a lesson, not a definition of who you are.*)
- **You stay consistent** because you respect yourself enough to follow through. (*Discipline isn't punishment—it's an act of self-respect.*)

Without Self-Love:

- **You chase goals out of fear**—fear of being left behind, fear of not being "good enough." (*Your motivation comes from insecurity, not inspiration.*)

- You see failure as a confirmation of your worst fears: *"Maybe I'm not cut out for this." (Instead of learning, you shut down.)*
- **You burn out easily** because you're running on stress, not self-respect. *(You push yourself out of fear, not because you truly want to.)*

The Shift: From Self-Criticism to Self-Compassion

The **biggest difference?**

When you love yourself, you don't let challenges define you—you let them refine you.

Self-love allows you to see **failure as feedback, not finality.** Self-love helps you stay **resilient instead of reactive.** Self-love keeps you moving forward—not because you're afraid to stop, but because you **believe in yourself.**

Exercise: Shift Your Perspective on Challenges

1. **Think about the last time you faced a challenge.**
- What was your **first reaction?** Did you feel **self-compassion** or **self-criticism?**
2. **Now, ask yourself:**
- *How would this have been different if I had given myself grace instead of pressure?*
- *What would I say to a friend in this situation—and why don't I say it to myself?*
3. **Write down one way you can shift your mindset next time.**

- How can you approach challenges with **kindness instead of judgment**?

Because when you truly love yourself? **You don't fight against yourself—you fight for yourself.**
And **that's how you win.**

2. The Truth About Motivation: It's Not About Forcing Yourself—It's About Understanding Yourself

Let's be real—**motivation is a myth.**

No one wakes up **inspired and energized every single day.** Even the most successful people **don't rely on motivation.**

What do they rely on?

Systems. (*They build routines that make progress automatic.*)

Habits. (*They create momentum so they don't have to "feel like it" to take action.*)

Self-awareness. (*They know what actually works for them and lean into it.*)

The secret? Motivation doesn't create action—action creates motivation.

Once you start, even in **small ways**, momentum takes over. But the key is making sure your **approach works for YOU.**

What Works for Someone Else Might Not Work for You

Some people **thrive on structure**—daily schedules, routines, and to-do lists keep them on track.

Others **thrive on flow**—they work best when they follow their energy and intuition.

Some people do their best work **early in the morning**, while others are **night owls** who hit their peak late at night.

The point? **Your best rhythm is unique to you.**

Instead of forcing yourself into **productivity methods that don't fit**, start learning **how you actually function best.**

Find Your Unique Balance

Ask yourself:

- **Do I work better with strict routines or flexible schedules?** (*Does a set structure help, or does it feel suffocating?*)
- **Do I need external accountability, or am I more independent?** (*Do deadlines and check-ins keep me motivated, or do I thrive on self-discipline?*)
- **Do I thrive under pressure, or do I perform best with ease and space?** (*Do I work well with tight deadlines, or do I need breathing room to do my best?*)

There's no right or wrong answer—only what's right for you.

When you stop **forcing yourself** into a productivity style that **doesn't align with your natural rhythm**, you stop **burning out—** and you start **thriving.**

Exercise: Tap Into Your Most Productive Energy

1. **Think about a time you felt the most productive and energized.**

1. What conditions made that possible? (*Were you working alone or with people? Was it structured or flexible?*)
2. **Write down what worked best for you.**
- What habits, routines, or settings helped you feel clear, focused, and energized?
3. **Now, ask yourself: How can you recreate that energy in your daily life?**
- What small changes can you make to work with yourself, instead of against yourself?

The Takeaway? Work With Yourself, Not Against Yourself.

You don't need to force productivity—you just need to understand your own rhythm.

You don't need to rely on motivation—you just need to build systems that keep you moving.

And once you start aligning with what works for you? You'll realize you never needed "motivation" in the first place.

3. Perfecting Your Brain's Algorithm to Work in Your Favor

Your mind is constantly running a **program**. And guess what? **You control the code.**

Every time you think a thought, you're reinforcing a **neural pathway** in your brain. The more you repeat it, the stronger it becomes—just like a well-worn path in the woods.

If you constantly tell yourself:

"I'm lazy."

"I can't focus."

"I always fail."

Your brain **accepts that as truth** and makes it your **default setting**.

But if you start telling yourself:

"I am capable."

"I am learning."

"I am figuring things out."

Your brain **starts building evidence** for that reality instead.

This isn't just **positive thinking.** This is **science.**

How to Reprogram Your Mental Algorithm

Just like **curating your social media feed,** you can **curate your thoughts and beliefs** so that your mind starts working **for you** instead of **against you.**

Reframe Negative Thoughts

When a **negative thought** pops up, don't just accept it—**challenge it.**

Instead of: *"I can't do this."*

Say: *"I'm still learning, but I'm getting better every day."*

Instead of: *"I always procrastinate."*

Say: *"I'm learning how to work in a way that suits me."*

Instead of: *"I'll never be successful."*

Say: *"Success is a process, and every step I take is progress."*

Your **brain listens to what you tell it.** Feed it thoughts that **empower you.**

Expose Yourself to the Right Inputs

Your **brain is shaped** by what you **consume daily.**

If you constantly surround yourself with:

- **Negative self-talk** (*from yourself or others*)
- **Toxic content** that makes you feel like you're behind
- **People who doubt you or drain your energy**

Then your brain **absorbs that reality** and makes it your **mental default.**

Curate your environment:

Follow people who inspire and uplift you.

Read books, listen to podcasts, and engage with content that elevates your mindset.

Surround yourself with people who **support your growth** instead of holding you back.

If you want your brain to work in your favor, **feed it the right fuel.**

Take Action, Even in Small Ways

Your brain **loves proof**—it thrives on **real-life evidence.**

Every time you **take action**, even in the smallest way, your brain registers it as **evidence that you are capable.**

Want to be more disciplined? Start with a **tiny habit** you can stick to daily. (*Even just making your bed can be a first step.*)

Want to be more confident? Start practicing **self-affirmations daily** (*Look in the mirror and tell yourself, "I've got this."*)

Want to overcome fear? Take a **small, courageous action** (*Send that email, start that project, set that boundary.*)

It's not about **big leaps**—it's about **consistent steps**.

Because every small action is **proof** that you're capable. And when your brain **sees proof, it believes it.**

Exercise: Rewire One Limiting Belief

1. **Think of one limiting belief you've been carrying.** (*Example: "I'm not good enough."*)
2. **Challenge it:** *Is this actually true, or is it just a fear-based thought?*
3. **Reframe it:** *What's a truth that supports you instead? (Example: "I am always learning, growing, and improving."*)
4. **Take one small action today** that reinforces this new belief.

Because the more you **train your brain to work for you**, the more unstoppable you become.

The Truth? You're Already Reprogramming Your Mind—Make Sure It's in the Right Direction.

Your thoughts are shaping your reality every day. You are not stuck—you are rewiring your brain with every new belief you choose. So choose thoughts that build you up, not break you down.

Final Thoughts: Self-Love Is About Working With Yourself, Not Against Yourself

Most of us are taught to **push, force, and grind** our way through life.

Work harder. Do more. Be better. Hustle non-stop.

But real success? **It doesn't come from burnout—it comes from alignment.**

The moment you stop **fighting yourself** and start **working with yourself**, everything shifts.

Your best way of working is unique to you. (*What works for others might not work for you—and that's okay.*)

Your path to success doesn't have to look like anyone else's. (*You are not behind. You are on YOUR timeline.*)

Your worth isn't determined by how productive you are—it's about how aligned you are. (*Self-love isn't about proving yourself— it's about trusting yourself.*)

The goal isn't to **"fix" yourself.**

It's to **understand yourself so deeply** that success becomes inevitable.

And that? That's the most powerful self-love practice of all.

Affirmation:

"I trust myself. I know my rhythm. I honor my process. Success flows when I work in alignment with who I truly am."

Chapter 7: Self-Love and the People You Surround Yourself With

Self-love isn't just about how you treat yourself—it's about the **energy you allow into your life.**

The people around you shape **your mindset, your confidence, your peace, and even your success.**

You could be doing **all the self-work in the world,** but if your circle is filled with:

Negativity (*people who drain you*)

Jealousy (*people who secretly resent you*)

Toxicity (*people who thrive on drama*)

Lack of support (*people who don't believe in you*)

Then no amount of self-care, affirmations, or journaling will make up for the **weight of a bad environment.**

The truth is, **you are a reflection of the people you spend the most time with.**

Your circle should:

Uplift you, not exhaust you.

Encourage your growth, not limit you.

Feel like a safe space, not a battlefield.

This chapter is all about **evaluating your relationships, protecting your energy, and surrounding yourself with the kind of people who align with your highest self.**

Because real self-love? **It includes knowing when to walk away.**

1. The Importance of Choosing the Right People

You've probably heard the saying:

"You are the average of the five people you spend the most time with."

At first, it might sound like just another motivational quote, but when you really think about it, **it's one of the most powerful truths about human nature.**

Your environment **shapes you**—whether you realize it or not. The people you surround yourself with influence:

The way you think.

The way you handle challenges.

The way you view your own potential.

Even the way you speak to yourself.

If you're spending time with people who **uplift you, inspire you, and challenge you to grow**, you're naturally going to evolve into the best version of yourself.

But if you're surrounded by people who **complain, doubt, or drain your energy**, that negativity will start to seep into your mindset, no matter how much self-work you do.

The truth is, **energy is contagious**—and you have to be intentional about what kind of energy you allow into your space.

If You're Constantly Around:

People who complain all the time → You'll start seeing the world through their lens of **negativity**. (*Suddenly, everything feels like a problem instead of an opportunity. You begin focusing on what's wrong instead of what's possible.*)

People who doubt themselves → You'll start **second-guessing yourself, too.** (*When you hear people constantly talk about how hard* life is, how nothing ever works out, and how they'll "never make it," those beliefs start embedding into your own mind.)

People who settle for less → You'll start thinking **maybe that's just how life is.** (*It becomes easy to lower your own expectations when no one around you is striving for more.*)

Think about it—if you spend every day with people who only see obstacles, you'll stop seeing opportunities.

Your circle becomes your **normal**—so if you're surrounded by **limiting energy**, it will **limit you.**

But When You're Surrounded By:

People who inspire you → You start believing **more is possible.** (*You absorb their mindset. Their wins remind you that success is achievable. Their ambition fuels yours.*)

People who take action → You feel motivated to **step up.** (*When you see people around you chasing goals, pushing through fear, and making things happen, you naturally start doing the same.*)

People who encourage you → You feel safe being **your best self.** (*You don't have to shrink, dim your light, or filter your excitement. You can fully step into your power without fear of judgment.*)

People who challenge you to grow → You level up faster than you ever thought possible. (*They call you out when you make excuses, push you to do better, and remind you what you're capable of.*)

The right people don't just **support you**—they **elevate you.**

Who's Really in Your Circle?

Take a second to think about the people in your life.

Who in your life makes you feel lighter, inspired, and aligned?

Who makes you feel drained, doubted, or stuck?

Who do you leave feeling energized, and who do you leave feeling exhausted?

Your energy **doesn't lie.** Pay attention to how you feel after spending time with people—it will tell you everything you need to know.

And remember: **You don't owe anyone unlimited access to your energy just because of history or obligation.**

Exercise: Audit Your Circle

Step 1: Write down the 5 people you spend the most time with. (*This could be friends, family, coworkers—whoever has the biggest impact on your energy.*)

Step 2: Next to each name, write how they make you feel:

- **Do they energize or drain you?**
- **Do they inspire or limit you?**
- **Do they encourage or discourage you?**

Step 3: Reflect on the results.

- If your circle **elevates you**, that's a sign you're in a **growth-oriented environment.**
- If your circle **weighs you down**, it may be time to **set boundaries, limit interactions, or seek new connections that align with your best self.**

Because **self-love means surrounding yourself with people who reflect the energy, growth, and joy you deserve.**

2. Protecting Your Energy from Negativity and Subconscious Jealousy (Evil Eye)

Not everyone who claps for you is happy for you.

Some people **pretend to be supportive**, but deep down, they're uncomfortable with your growth. Sometimes it's **silent jealousy**, sometimes it's **hidden resentment**, and sometimes it's just their own **limiting beliefs projecting onto you.**

They may not even **realize** they're doing it. But **energy never lies.**

Signs of Subconscious Jealousy & Energy Draining People

The Friend Who "Jokes" About Your Growth

- *"Oh, look who suddenly thinks they're successful."* (*Passive-aggressive shade disguised as humor.*)
- *"You're so lucky, I wish things just fell into place for me too."* (*Undermining your hard work by calling it luck.*)

The One Who Can't Celebrate You Without Making It About Themselves

- You share a **win**, and suddenly they're venting about their own struggles.
- Instead of **genuinely celebrating you**, they shift the attention back onto themselves.
- Their energy says: *"Yeah, but what about ME?"*

The One Who Only Likes You When You're Struggling

- When you're **going through it**, they're **there for you**. (*Because it makes them feel superior.*)

- But the moment you **start thriving**, they **act distant, bitter, or uninterested.**
- They were **comfortable when you weren't doing better than them.**

Energy vampires are real. And if you **feel drained, doubted, or diminished** after being around someone, **pay attention.**

How to Protect Your Energy

Trust your gut.

- If someone's **energy feels off**, don't **ignore it.**
- If you always leave interactions **feeling small or uncertain**, that's your **intuition telling you something.**

Limit access.

- **Not everyone needs to know your moves.**
- Keep things **private until they're solid.** *Your success doesn't need an audience before it's ready.*

Stop seeking approval.

- The more you **rely on people's validation**, the easier it is for **their energy to influence you.**
- Be confident in **your own path**—whether people understand it or not.

Use discernment.

- Just because someone has been in your life for **years** doesn't mean they deserve a **front-row seat in your future.**
- Some people are meant to be **part of your past, not your destiny.**

Exercise: Spot the Energy Shift
1. Think of a time you shared exciting news and someone's reaction felt... off.
2. How did it make you feel? (*Did they celebrate you? Did they dismiss you? Did they get distant?*)
3. What does that tell you about their energy? (*Were they genuinely happy for you, or did their energy shift when you started thriving?*)

Because **real friends celebrate you—not just when you're struggling, but when you're winning, too.**

3. How People Subtly Hold You Back (And How to Break Free)

Not everyone who **holds you back** does it on purpose.

Sometimes, they don't even realize they're **projecting their own fears, insecurities, or limiting beliefs** onto you.

But if you're not careful, their doubts can become **your doubts.** Their fears can become **your fears.** Their limitations can start **defining your potential.**

And that's why **self-love means protecting yourself—not just from obvious negativity, but from subtle, sneaky energy that keeps you stuck.**

How People Subtly Hold You Back

Note that these are all examples of possibilities. Just because someone uses the following phrases with you, it doesn't mean they could be trying to hold you back. They could have a genuine concern. You need to be able to tell the difference based on your intuition as well as the experiences you have with the person.

The Doubter:

"Are you sure that's a good idea?"

"That seems risky. Maybe you should play it safe."

Translation: *"I don't believe in myself enough to take risks, so I don't want you to either."*

They might **think they're looking out for you**, but really, they're **pushing their own fears onto you.**

The Guilt-Tripper:

"You've changed."

"You're too busy for me now."

Translation: *"I liked you better when you weren't growing past me."*

They're uncomfortable with your **evolution**, so they try to **shame you into staying the same.**

The Dream Crusher:

"Not everyone can be successful."

"You're being unrealistic."

Translation: *"I gave up on my dreams, so I don't want to see you achieve yours."*

They settled, so they **want you to settle too.** Instead of working on their own growth, they try to **convince you that yours is impossible.**

Here's the Truth:

People will **project their limitations onto you if you let them.**

But **self-love means choosing yourself, even when it makes others uncomfortable.**

Because the people who are **truly for you** will never try to **convince you to be less.**

How to Break Free from People Who Hold You Back

Set Boundaries.

- You don't have to **cut people off immediately**, but you do need to **create distance.**
- Protect your energy by being **intentional** about how much time and space you give them.

Stop Explaining Yourself.

- You don't need to **justify your growth** to anyone.
- The right people won't **need an explanation**—they'll just **support you.**

Surround Yourself with Expanders.

- Find people who **push you, inspire you, and remind you of your potential.**
- Look for those who have already **broken through their own limitations**—they'll help you do the same.

Protect Your Peace Relentlessly.

- If someone's **energy feels heavy**, trust that feeling.
- Your peace is **not up for negotiation.**

The Shift: Owning Your Power

When you stop **shrinking to make others comfortable**, you finally step into your **full power.**

You no longer **absorb other people's doubts**—you trust your own vision.

You no longer **let guilt hold you back**—you honor your own growth.

You no longer **ask for permission to evolve**—you just **evolve.**

Exercise: Reclaim Your Energy

1. **Think of someone whose doubts or negativity have influenced you.** (*Whose voice has made you second-guess yourself?*)
2. **What boundaries can you set to protect your energy?** (*Less time with them? Less sharing? More emotional distance?*)
3. **What's one action you can take today to fully choose yourself?** (*A decision, a mindset shift, a commitment to stop seeking approval?*)

Because at the end of the day, **self-love means refusing to live a life that keeps you small.**

And **you are not small.**

Affirmation:

"I only allow people into my life who align with my highest self. My energy is sacred, and I protect it fiercely."

Chapter 8: Red Flags vs. Green Flags – Know the Difference, Protect Your Peace

Loving yourself means protecting yourself. And one of the biggest ways to do that? *Knowing the difference between red flags and green flags in relationships.*

And let's be clear—this isn't just about romance.

Red flags aren't just relationship drama or "bad moments." They're warning signs that someone—whether a partner, friend, family member, or coworker—is not aligned with your well-being. They show you when a dynamic is draining, disrespectful, or unsafe.

Green flags aren't just "nice traits." They're the foundation of *every* healthy, secure connection. They tell you when a relationship—romantic, platonic, professional, or familial—is built on trust, respect, and emotional maturity.

This applies to *every* relationship in your life.

- A friend who guilt-trips you and makes you feel bad for setting boundaries? **Red flag.**
- A family member who respects your choices without judgment? **Green flag.**
- A coworker who undermines you but pretends they're joking? **Red flag.**
- A partner who communicates openly and supports your growth? **Green flag.**

When you start recognizing **red flags early**, you stop making excuses for toxic behavior.

When you start recognizing **green flags**, you learn what *real* support and respect actually look like.

And when you trust yourself enough to *act* on what you see? *You protect your energy, your peace, and your future.*

This chapter is about learning to see the difference—so you can choose relationships that *lift you up* instead of drain you.

1. Red Flags: Warning Signs That Someone is Not Aligned With Your Well-Being

Red flags are not "one-time mistakes." They're patterns. Recurring behaviors. Clues that someone isn't emotionally safe to have in your life. It's easy to overlook them when you're hopeful about a relationship, but ignoring red flags never makes them disappear—it just gives them time to grow into something bigger.

Red flags don't always scream; sometimes, they whisper. They show up in the little things—dismissive comments, guilt-tripping disguised as "concern," inconsistent behavior that leaves you second-guessing yourself. And the hardest part? They can be easy to excuse in the moment.

Maybe you told yourself they "didn't mean it that way." Maybe you thought they'd change. Maybe you wanted to believe that the good parts of the relationship outweighed the bad. But when someone consistently disregards your feelings, your needs, and your well-being, that's not love—it's misalignment.

If you notice these behaviors, pay attention. Your peace is too valuable to sacrifice for the sake of giving someone the benefit of the doubt.

Common Red Flags in Any Relationship:

Lack of Accountability – They never take responsibility for their actions. Instead, they always have an excuse, a justification, or someone else to blame. They might even flip the script and make you feel like *you* did something wrong just for bringing it up. If someone can't own up to their mistakes, how can they grow? More importantly, how can they be in a healthy relationship with you?

Gaslighting – They make you question your own feelings or reality. If you bring up something that hurt you, they tell you, "You're overreacting," or "That never happened." They twist situations until you start doubting yourself, and before you know it, you're apologizing for things that weren't your fault.

Love Bombing – At first, they seem *perfect*. Over-the-top affection, excessive compliments, constant attention—so much that it feels almost too good to be true. And then the shift happens. The same person who showered you with love starts using it as a tool—guilt-tripping you, controlling you, or suddenly pulling away to keep you chasing the version of them they showed you in the beginning.

Inconsistency – One day they're all in, the next they're distant. They text you all the time for a week, then disappear. They make plans and cancel last minute. Their energy is unpredictable, leaving you on edge, trying to figure out where you stand with them. A connection that makes you feel emotionally unstable is not a safe one.

Passive-Aggressive Behavior – Instead of communicating openly, they use sarcasm, backhanded compliments, guilt trips, or the silent treatment to punish you. Healthy relationships require *direct* communication—if someone refuses to have honest conversations but has no problem making you feel bad, that's a problem.

Disrespecting Boundaries – They push your limits, dismiss your needs, or make you feel guilty for having boundaries in the first place. If you say you need space, they accuse you of being distant. If you say no to something, they try to wear you down until you say yes. Someone who doesn't respect your boundaries does not respect *you*.

Jealousy & Competition – Instead of celebrating your wins, they make it about them. Instead of supporting your growth, they subtly (or not so subtly) try to one-up you. They don't clap for you unless they feel like they're ahead of you. That's not love—that's rivalry disguised as a relationship.

Guilt-Tripping & Manipulation – They use your kindness against you. If you try to stand up for yourself, they make you feel guilty. If you say no, they act hurt. If you express a concern, they twist it until *you're* the bad guy. Relationships should be built on mutual respect, not emotional games.

Reminder: A red flag doesn't mean someone is a "bad person." It doesn't mean they don't have good qualities. But it does mean that they are not emotionally safe for you. You are not responsible for fixing them, saving them, or enduring their behavior just because you see their potential. Potential means nothing without action.

Reflection Exercise:
- Have you ever ignored a red flag?
- Looking back, what was the first sign that something felt off?
- What did you tell yourself at the time to justify it?
- How did things turn out in the end?

The truth is, your intuition *always* speaks to you. The real question is: are you listening?

2. Green Flags: Signs of a Healthy, Supportive Dynamic

Green flags are the real flex. They don't just show you who's safe—they show you what *healthy* looks like. While red flags are warning signs that someone is misaligned with your well-being, green flags are the markers of security, emotional intelligence, and genuine connection. These are the people who don't drain you, confuse you, or make you question your worth. Instead, they add value to your life simply by being in it.

A person who is emotionally mature, self-aware, and secure doesn't need to manipulate, guilt-trip, or play power games. They don't make love conditional or friendships transactional. They show up for you not just when it's convenient for them, but because they genuinely care.

The beauty of green flags is that they *feel easy*. If you feel calm, safe, and valued in someone's presence, pay attention—that's a sign you're experiencing a relationship built on mutual respect and trust.

Common Green Flags in Any Relationship:

Emotional Maturity – They own their mistakes, communicate openly, and handle conflict with respect. They don't resort to passive-aggressive behavior or avoid difficult conversations just because they're uncomfortable. Instead, they work *with* you, not against you, to find solutions.

Consistency – Their actions match their words. They don't make promises they can't keep, and they don't leave you questioning where you stand with them. With consistent people, there's no second-guessing, no mixed signals—just stability.

Respect for Boundaries – They understand that "no" is a complete sentence. They respect your space, your time, and your limits without trying to guilt you into changing them. They don't take your boundaries personally because they understand that healthy relationships require mutual respect.

Active Listening – They don't just wait for their turn to talk; they *hear* you. They remember things that matter to you, ask thoughtful questions, and make you feel understood. You don't have to fight for their attention because they genuinely care about what you have to say.

Accountability – They don't blame others when they mess up. Instead, they take full responsibility, apologize sincerely, and make real efforts to improve. They don't just say, "I'm sorry"—they show you through changed behavior.

Mutual Support – They don't just clap for you when you succeed; they *genuinely* celebrate your wins. They uplift your dreams, encourage your growth, and don't feel threatened by your success. Their support is real, not performative.

Emotional Safety – You don't have to walk on eggshells around them. You feel at peace in their presence, not anxious or on edge. You can express yourself freely without fear of being judged, ridiculed, or manipulated. A safe person *feels* safe.

Reciprocity – The energy, effort, and care in the relationship feel balanced. You're not the only one initiating conversations, making plans, or giving support—it's a two-way street. Healthy relationships don't feel like emotional labor; they feel like mutual investment.

Reminder: Green flags feel easy. There's no chasing, no confusion, no emotional rollercoaster—just natural, steady, mutual care. Healthy relationships aren't built on adrenaline or intensity; they're built on trust, understanding, and respect.

Reflection Exercise:

- Think of someone in your life who is a green flag.
- What qualities make them a safe and healthy presence?
- How does being around them *feel* compared to relationships that drained you?

Surrounding yourself with green-flag people doesn't just make life easier—it reminds you what you deserve.

3. How to Trust Your Intuition When Something Feels Off

You *always* know.

Even when you ignore it. Even when you try to reason with yourself. Even when you give someone the benefit of the doubt for the tenth time—your gut already told you everything you needed to know.

The problem isn't that your intuition is unclear. It's that you've been conditioned to second-guess it. You've been taught to be "understanding," to "give people a chance," to be polite even when something in you is screaming *this isn't right.*

Ignoring your intuition is how you end up in situations you should have avoided.

Your intuition is *not* paranoia. It's not irrational. It's not something you need to silence. It's your built-in protection system, designed to keep you safe, and the more you trust it, the stronger it becomes.

Pay Attention To:

Your body's reaction. Do you feel tight, drained, or anxious around someone? Do you suddenly get a headache, stomach discomfort, or an uneasy feeling for no reason? That's your intuition speaking through your body. Your nervous system picks up on energy before your mind can fully process it. If your body feels uncomfortable, don't dismiss it.

Patterns, not words. Anyone can say the right things, but actions reveal *everything*. If someone's behavior contradicts their words, believe the behavior. If they constantly "didn't mean it that way" but keep doing the same thing? Believe the pattern, not the excuse.

The energy shift. Some people leave you feeling lighter, inspired, and safe. Others leave you feeling drained, confused, or uneasy. If you always feel worse after interacting with someone, don't ignore that feeling. Energy doesn't lie.

How to Strengthen Your Intuition:

Stop justifying or over-explaining your feelings. You don't need a long list of reasons to trust your gut. "Something feels off" is enough.

Take a step back and observe. Instead of reacting emotionally, sit with what you're feeling. What's making you uncomfortable? What patterns have you noticed?

Set boundaries as soon as something feels off. Don't wait for more proof. You don't need someone to *officially* hurt you before protecting your peace. If something feels misaligned, you have the right to distance yourself.

Reflection Exercise:
Think of a time your intuition was right.

- How did your body react?
- What signs did you ignore?
- How can you trust yourself more moving forward?

The more you listen to yourself, the more confident you become in your own judgment. Your intuition is not here to ruin your fun—it's here to *save* you from unnecessary pain. Trust it. It already knows.

4. Why We Ignore Red Flags (And How to Stop)

Let's be real—people don't ignore red flags because they "don't see them." They ignore them because acknowledging them means facing an uncomfortable truth. And sometimes, that truth is hard to accept.

Maybe it's the fear of losing someone. Maybe it's the hope that things will magically get better. Maybe it's the belief that walking away means "giving up." Whatever the reason, ignoring red flags never makes them go away—it just delays the inevitable.

So, why do we do it?

The Most Common Reasons People Ignore Red Flags:

Low Self-Worth – *"Maybe I don't deserve better."* If deep down you don't believe you're worthy of a healthy, fulfilling relationship, you might settle for less without even realizing it. You might think, *This is just how relationships are* or *At least they love me in their own way.* But love that comes at the cost of your peace is not love—it's self-sacrifice.

Fear of Being Alone – *"I'd rather have this than nothing at all."* Loneliness can be a powerful force. It can make you convince yourself that *any* connection is better than none. But let me tell you something: *Being alone is better than being with the wrong people.* Nothing drains your spirit faster than staying in a situation that depletes you just because you're afraid of what's on the other side of leaving.

Hoping They'll Change – *"Maybe they'll be different for me."* People don't change unless *they* want to. No amount of love, patience, or effort can force someone to grow if they're not willing to do the work themselves. You are not a rehabilitation center for emotionally unavailable people. You are not here to fix, heal, or wait for someone to become what you need.

Societal Conditioning – *"Relationships take work—I shouldn't expect perfection."* We've been taught that relationships require effort, compromise, and patience—and that's true. But effort is a two-way street, and *compromise should never mean compromising yourself.* There's a difference between working through minor challenges and tolerating toxic behavior under the excuse that "nobody's perfect."

But Here's the Truth:

Your **self-worth** is not up for debate.

Being alone is better than being with the wrong people.

You are **not here to fix, heal, or wait** for someone to change.

Having standards doesn't mean you're "too picky"—it means you respect yourself.

And the biggest truth of all?

You don't have to justify why you don't want someone in your life. If a person makes you feel unsafe, unfulfilled, or drained, *that is reason enough to walk away.*

Reflection Exercise:

- Have you ever justified staying in a situation that wasn't good for you?
- Why did you stay?
- What lesson did you learn?

Growth comes when you start honoring your own boundaries. The more you trust yourself, the less tolerance you'll have for anything that disrupts your peace.

5. How to Cultivate Green Flag Relationships

Here's the truth: *You don't just attract green flag relationships—you create them by embodying the same energy you want to receive.*

If you want relationships that are safe, fulfilling, and supportive, it starts with *you*. The healthiest connections don't come from luck or wishful thinking—they come from alignment. When you show up as someone who is emotionally mature, self-aware, and intentional in your relationships, you naturally start attracting and keeping people who match that energy.

So instead of asking, *"Where are all the green flag people?"* ask yourself:

Am I showing up as the kind of person I want to attract?

Because energy doesn't lie. When you hold yourself to a certain standard, the people who can't meet it naturally fall away, and the ones who can will gravitate toward you.

How to Attract Green Flag People:

Be consistent. People feel safe around consistency. When your actions match your words, when you follow through on what you say, and when you show up in a steady, reliable way—you attract others who do the same.

Communicate honestly. Say what you mean, and mean what you say. Green flag relationships thrive on *clear, open, and direct* communication. You don't play games, manipulate, or leave people guessing where they stand with you.

Take accountability. Nobody is perfect, and that's okay. But the difference between a green flag person and a red flag person? *Accountability.* When you mess up, you own it. You don't shift blame, make excuses, or gaslight. You learn, you grow, and you do better.

Be supportive. Healthy relationships are built on *mutual upliftment.* You don't compete with the people around you—you celebrate them. You want to see them win, and they want the same for you. Real connection is never a competition.

Set boundaries. If you don't protect your energy, you'll attract people who don't respect it. Having strong boundaries means you value your own well-being, and when you respect yourself, you naturally attract people who do too.

The Secret to Finding Green Flag Relationships:

When you become the type of person you want to attract, you naturally start aligning with the right people.

You don't have to chase them. You don't have to wonder why you keep attracting the wrong ones. The right people recognize each other, and when you live with integrity, self-respect, and emotional intelligence, those same qualities will find their way into your relationships.

Reflection Exercise:

- What's one green flag trait you want to embody more in your relationships?
- How can you start practicing it in your daily interactions?

The best relationships start with *who you are first.*

6. When Is It a Red Flag vs. Just Who They Are?

Not every "red flag" means someone is toxic. Sometimes, it's just a personality trait, a difference in communication styles, or a habit that *bothers you* but doesn't actually harm the relationship.

The reality is, *nobody is perfect.* Everyone has flaws, quirks, and moments of emotional immaturity—including you. The key is learning how to recognize the difference between a true red flag that threatens your well-being and something that's just *part of who they are.*

Here's the question to ask yourself:
Is this a dealbreaker, or just a difference?

How to Tell the Difference:

Red flags affect your well-being. If a behavior makes you feel drained, anxious, unsafe, or constantly disrespected—it's a red flag.

Personality quirks are just things that might annoy you. Maybe they're always late. Maybe they don't text back quickly. Maybe they talk too much about a hobby you don't care about. Annoying? Yes. Toxic? No.

Red flags are repeated behaviors that show a lack of emotional safety. If someone keeps crossing your boundaries, manipulating you, or making you question your worth, that's a pattern—not a personality trait.

Personality traits are neutral—whether they bother you depends on compatibility. For example, being introverted isn't a red flag. Neither is being blunt or having a dry sense of humor. But if those traits make you feel ignored or disrespected, that's when you have to decide whether the relationship *as a whole* works for you.

Deciding When to Let Something Go

Nobody in your life is going to be 100% perfect. The goal isn't to cut off everyone who isn't ideal—it's to *discern what truly matters.* There's a difference between protecting your peace and holding people to impossible standards.

Let's be real: *Everyone has something that could be considered a "red flag" to someone.* Maybe they're terrible at texting back. Maybe they're awkward with emotions. Maybe they joke too much when you want a serious conversation. The question is—does it actually matter in the bigger picture? Or is it just a quirk that's part of who they are?

Instead of immediately labeling something as a dealbreaker, take a step back and reflect:

Ask Yourself:

1. Does this behavior actually harm me, or is it just something I find frustrating?

- Annoying ≠ toxic. A friend who always runs late might drive you crazy, but that's not the same as a friend who constantly disrespects your time by canceling last minute or making you feel unimportant.
- If it *affects your well-being*, it's worth addressing. If it's just an occasional annoyance, ask yourself if it's something you can live with.

2. Does this person add more value to my life than stress?

- Nobody is going to be *perfect*, but the right people should bring more joy, support, and security than frustration.
- If their presence in your life feels overwhelmingly negative, exhausting, or draining, that's a problem. But if their good qualities far outweigh the occasional irritation, it might be something worth letting go.

3. If I were to bring this up, would they try to improve, or dismiss my feelings?

- Healthy relationships allow space for growth. If someone genuinely respects you, they will at least *consider* your feelings, even if they don't change overnight.

- The real red flag isn't the behavior itself—it's the unwillingness to *listen, acknowledge, and try*. If someone refuses to even *hear you out*, that's when you know it's not just a personality trait—it's a lack of care.

The Bottom Line: Weigh the Whole Picture

Nobody is just *one thing*. A person isn't just *their bad habits* or *their best moments*—they're the sum of everything they bring to your life. The key is figuring out whether the **full picture** of this person aligns with what you need and deserve.

If someone genuinely **respects you, communicates well, and consistently shows up for you**, a small "red flag" might just be a difference that you learn to accept.

If their behavior **consistently hurts you and they refuse to change**, *that's* when it's a real red flag.

The power is in *your* hands. You don't have to settle, but you also don't have to cut off everyone for every little flaw. It's about choosing the people who bring out the best in you—flaws and all.

Final Thoughts: Protect Your Peace Like Your Life Depends on It (Because It Does)

At the end of the day, *your peace is your responsibility*. Who you allow in your life—who you give your time, energy, and emotions to—directly affects your well-being. And the more you love yourself, the easier it becomes to choose relationships that *nourish* you instead of drain you.

Red flags are not challenges to overcome—they are warnings to walk away. Love, friendship, or any kind of connection should never feel like a constant uphill battle. You don't need to prove your worth, earn someone's respect, or keep giving second chances to people who repeatedly show you they are not safe.

Green flags are not "rare"—they are the standard you should expect. Healthy, supportive, and fulfilling relationships are not unicorns. They exist, and they are *available to you*. But you have to stop accepting bare minimum behavior as if it's all you can get. The standard you set is the standard you receive.

Your intuition is not optional—it is your built-in protection system. Ignoring your intuition never leads to a good outcome. The signs are always there, but it's up to you to trust yourself enough to act on them. The moment something feels off, *listen*. If you feel unsafe, unheard, or unfulfilled in a relationship, *that is reason enough to leave.*

The more you prioritize your peace, the more naturally everything else falls into place. The right people won't feel like an emotional rollercoaster. The right relationships won't leave you drained. And the right love—whether romantic, platonic, or within yourself—will feel like home.

You are worthy of relationships that feel safe, easy, and secure. Never settle for less.

Affirmation: *"I trust my intuition. I recognize red flags and walk away. I attract and align with relationships that are healthy, safe, and supportive."*

Chapter 9: That's a You Problem – Stop Taking on Other People's Baggage

Let's get something straight—you are not a therapist, a savior, or an emotional dumping ground. *Your role in life is not to absorb other people's problems until you're drained, exhausted, and carrying weight that was never yours to bear.*

Yes, having empathy is a gift. Yes, being a good listener is valuable. But *there is a difference between being supportive and being someone's emotional sponge.* There is a fine line between being there for people and losing yourself in their chaos.

Some people will mistake your kindness for an invitation to offload all their emotional baggage onto you. They will call you only when they need something, treat you like a free therapist, or dump their problems on you without ever asking how you're doing. And before you know it, you're exhausted—mentally, emotionally, spiritually—carrying burdens that aren't even yours.

So let's be clear about a few things:

Not everyone deserves unlimited access to your emotional energy.

Not every problem is yours to solve.

Not every crisis is your responsibility to fix.

And **that's okay.**

Saying "no" doesn't make you selfish. Setting boundaries doesn't mean you don't care. Walking away from someone else's mess doesn't make you a bad person—it makes you *a person who values your own peace.*

This chapter is about recognizing the difference between *supporting people* and *carrying their problems*, learning how to set boundaries without guilt, and finally letting go of the urge to "fix" others.

Because the truth is? Some people don't actually want solutions—they just want someone to unload their baggage onto. And that? *That's a them problem, not a you problem.*

1. The Difference Between Empathy and Emotional Dumping

Being kind-hearted doesn't mean being a 24/7 emotional sponge. *You are not required to carry every emotional weight that gets handed to you.* There's a **big** difference between *healthy emotional support* and *being someone's emotional landfill.*

Empathy is a beautiful thing. It allows us to connect, understand, and be there for the people we care about. But **there's a limit**—and when that limit is crossed, what was once kindness turns into emotional exhaustion.

Empathy is:

Holding space for someone without letting their emotions consume you. You can listen, validate, and offer support *without absorbing their pain as your own.*

Offering support without sacrificing your own mental health. Being there for others should never mean abandoning *yourself.*

Understanding what someone is going through *without making it your responsibility to fix it.* You can care deeply about someone's struggles while still recognizing that *their healing is their responsibility, not yours.*

Emotional dumping is:

Someone constantly unloading their problems onto you without considering your emotional space. Every conversation feels like a therapy session you never signed up for.

Expecting you to be available at all times to listen, comfort, or give advice. They never check in on you—only reach out when they need something.

Leaving conversations feeling drained, anxious, or emotionally heavy. You didn't ask to carry all of this, but somehow, you leave the interaction feeling responsible for their entire life.

Reminder:

It is **not selfish** to protect your energy.

You are **not a bad person** for having boundaries.

Your emotional well-being matters just as much as theirs.

Real, healthy relationships involve **mutual emotional support**—not one person constantly carrying the weight while the other dumps.

Reflection Exercise:

- Think of someone in your life who constantly unloads their problems onto you.
- Do they ever ask how *you* feel?
- Do they respect your emotional boundaries, or is it always about them?

If you feel like you're always giving but never receiving emotional support, it might be time to set some boundaries.

2. Recognizing When People Project Their Problems Onto You

Not every criticism, opinion, or reaction is actually about you.

A lot of people are walking around with unhealed wounds—and instead of facing their own issues, they *project* them onto others. They take their own fears, insecurities, and unresolved emotions and throw them in your direction, as if making you feel bad will somehow fix what's broken in them.

And if you're not careful, you might start believing it. You might start questioning yourself, wondering, *Did I do something wrong?* When in reality, their reaction has *nothing* to do with you and *everything* to do with their own inner turmoil.

Signs Someone is Projecting Onto You:

They assume your actions have the same motives as theirs.

Example: They feel insecure about their accomplishments, so they assume that *you* must be trying to make them feel small—when in reality, you're just existing.

They make you feel guilty for their own choices.

Example: They make bad decisions, and instead of taking responsibility, they turn it around on you: *"If you were there for me more, I wouldn't be in this situation."*

They lash out at you for things that have nothing to do with you.

Example: They're angry at their boss, their ex, or their own life choices, but instead of dealing with it, they take it out on you— *because you're "too lucky," "too confident," or "don't get it."*

They criticize you for things they struggle with themselves.

Example: Someone who constantly gossips accuses you of being fake. Someone who can't commit to anything calls you inconsistent. People often attack others for the very things they can't handle in themselves.

Reminder:

When someone tries to make you responsible for their emotions, *that's a them problem.*

You do **not** have to carry their baggage.

You do **not** have to shrink yourself to make them feel better.

You do **not** have to take on blame that isn't yours.

If someone is projecting, *let them deal with it.* Their wounds are *not* your weight to carry.

Reflection Exercise:

- Think of a time someone projected their emotions onto you.
- How did it affect you?
- How can you stop letting other people's baggage weigh you down?

The more you recognize projection for what it is, the less power it has over you.

3. Setting Boundaries Without Guilt

Let's be real—*setting boundaries makes some people uncomfortable.*

Why? Because they're used to having unlimited access to you. They're used to you always picking up the phone, always saying yes, always putting their needs ahead of yours. They're used to dumping their problems on you without a second thought about how it affects *you.*

But guess what? **That's not your problem.**

If someone gets upset because you're setting a boundary, that's a sign that *the boundary was necessary in the first place.*

Healthy Boundaries Are an Act of Self-Love.

Boundaries aren't about pushing people away—they're about teaching people *how to treat you.* They protect your time, your energy, and your emotional well-being.

And the right people? They won't just *accept* your boundaries—they'll *appreciate* them.

How to Set Boundaries Without Feeling Guilty:

You don't have to answer every text immediately.

You are *not* an on-call therapist. Just because someone reaches out doesn't mean you have to drop everything to respond.

You don't have to be available 24/7.

Just because someone *needs* to vent doesn't mean you're *obligated* to listen. Their urgency is *not* your responsibility.

You can say, "I can't take this on right now."

That's *not* selfish—that's emotional self-care. Your well-being matters just as much as theirs.

You don't need to explain yourself.

"I don't have the capacity for this conversation right now" is a *full sentence.* You don't owe anyone a long explanation for prioritizing yourself.

Reminder:

People who **respect you** will respect your boundaries. People who **don't**? They only valued what you could *give* them—not *you.*

Let that sink in.

Reflection Exercise:

- What's *one* boundary you need to set with someone in your life?
- How can you start enforcing it *today*?

The more you honor your boundaries, the more peace you create in your life.

4. How to Let Go of the Need to "Fix" Others

Let's be honest—you can't save people who *don't want* to be saved.

Read that again.

It doesn't matter how much you love them.

It doesn't matter how much advice you give.

It doesn't matter how much you see their potential.

People change when THEY decide to change—not when you want them to.

And that's one of the hardest lessons to accept—because when you care about someone, it's natural to want to help. To give advice. To *push* them toward the better version of themselves that you know they could be.

But at some point, you have to realize: **You can't want it more than they do.**

No amount of love, patience, or effort can force someone to heal, grow, or take responsibility for their life if they're not ready. And constantly trying to "fix" someone? That's not help—that's self-sacrifice.

Shift Your Role: Support, Not Save

You are *not* responsible for saving people from themselves.

Your job: Support, *not save.*

Your role: Inspire, *not fix.*

Your responsibility: Protect your peace, *not carry someone else's chaos.*

How to Stop Trying to "Fix" People:
Recognize that you are not responsible for their healing.

- Their journey is *theirs* to take. You can offer guidance, but you are not their lifeline.

Detach from the outcome.

- It's *not your job* to make sure they succeed—it's *theirs.* You can support them, but they have to do the work.

Let go of guilt.

- You *didn't cause* their struggles, and it's *not your burden* to carry. You can love someone without making their pain your own.

Redirect that energy back to yourself.

- You can't pour into someone else when you're running on empty. Imagine what you could do if you put *that* energy into your own growth instead.

Reminder:

Just because you *care* doesn't mean you have to *carry*. Some people don't want solutions—they just want an audience.

You are allowed to step back. You are allowed to let go. You are allowed to stop exhausting yourself for people who *refuse* to help themselves.

Reflection Exercise:

- Think of someone you've been trying to "fix" or help endlessly.
- How would it feel to *let go* and allow them to take responsibility for their own life?

The moment you stop trying to fix others, you free yourself to focus on what truly matters—you.

Final Thoughts: Protecting Your Energy is Self-Respect

Self-love isn't just about affirmations and bubble baths—it's about *choosing yourself* even when it's hard. Even when people guilt-trip you. Even when setting boundaries makes others uncomfortable.

You are NOT responsible for carrying other people's emotional baggage.

You are NOT required to fix people who don't want to fix themselves.

You ARE allowed to set boundaries that protect your peace.

And you *don't* have to feel guilty for saying, *"That's a you problem."*

Because your energy? *It's too valuable to be wasted on people who drain it.*

At the end of the day, protecting your peace isn't selfish—it's *necessary.* The right people will respect your boundaries, appreciate your presence, and never expect you to sacrifice your well-being for them.

Choose yourself. Prioritize your peace. Never apologize for it.

Affirmation:

"I release the need to carry other people's burdens. I set boundaries with confidence. My energy is sacred, and I protect it without guilt."

Chapter 10: Soft Life, Hard Boundaries

Let's be clear—*self-love isn't just spa days, vacations, and face masks.*

It's not just the "feel-good" moments. It's not just treating yourself when you're exhausted. **Real self-love is about protecting your peace, creating balance, and refusing to let stress be your default setting.**

That's where the **soft life** comes in.

The soft life is about choosing *ease* over unnecessary struggle. It's about creating a life that *flows* instead of one that constantly drains you. But let's get one thing straight—*soft doesn't mean weak.*

Living a soft life doesn't mean being lazy, unmotivated, or avoiding responsibilities. It means:

Setting hard boundaries to protect your energy.

Letting go of toxic "hustle culture" that glorifies burnout.

Prioritizing your well-being without guilt.

Because what's the point of success, relationships, or even self-care if you're **constantly stressed, exhausted, or overextended?**

If you want a **soft life**, you need **hard boundaries.**

1. Why Self-Love Isn't Just Spa Days—It's About Protecting Your Peace

Self-care is great, but what's the point of taking a bubble bath if you're still saying *yes* to things that drain you? What's the point of treating yourself to a massage if you're constantly overbooking your schedule? What's the point of a "self-care" day if you're using it just to *recover* from a life that's running you into the ground?

Let's be real—self-love is not about temporary relief.

Self-love is not about escaping your stress—it's about **eliminating unnecessary stress in the first place.**

Too many people treat self-care like a *Band-Aid* when what they really need is a complete reset. If you're constantly needing to "unwind" or "recover," that's a sign that something is out of balance. Instead of using self-care to *cope*, what if you started using it to *prevent* burnout in the first place?

What Self-Love ISN'T:

Overbooking yourself and then needing a "self-care" day just to recover.

- If you're always running on empty, adding a face mask on top of exhaustion isn't going to fix it. You need boundaries, not just bubble baths.

Putting others before yourself 24/7 and then wondering why you're exhausted.

- If you constantly pour into everyone else but leave nothing for yourself, *that's not selflessness—that's self-neglect.*

Letting people drain your energy because you "don't want to be mean."

- Boundaries are not mean. Saying no is not mean. *Protecting your peace is not mean.*

What Self-Love IS:

Saying no to things that don't serve you—without guilt.

- You don't owe anyone an explanation for prioritizing your well-being.

Creating a life where you don't feel the need to "recover" all the time.

- Self-love isn't about temporary fixes. It's about designing a lifestyle that *sustains* your peace.

Protecting your peace like it's your most valuable asset—because it is.

- Your energy is currency. Stop spending it on things that don't give you anything in return.

Reminder:

If you're constantly needing to "escape" your life, **it's a sign something needs to change.**

Self-care is not just an *event*—it's a *way of living*. It's not about hitting a breaking point and then trying to heal—it's about creating a life where you don't constantly feel like you need to escape.

Reflection Exercise:

- Write down or think of **one thing** in your life that drains your energy.
- How can you set a boundary to change it?

Self-love isn't about recovering from chaos—it's about making sure the chaos never takes over in the first place.

2. The Soft Life Movement – Why Prioritizing Ease Isn't Laziness

There's a huge misconception that if you're not grinding 24/7, you're being lazy. But *who told you that struggle is the only path to success?*

The soft life isn't about avoiding hard work—it's about working *in alignment.* It's about making choices that don't drain you, pursuing success without burning yourself out, and refusing to wear exhaustion as a badge of honor.

Because let's be real—**hustle culture is a scam.**

It will have you believing that if you're not constantly *tired, overwhelmed, or busy,* you're somehow not *doing enough.* It will make you feel guilty for resting, as if you have to *earn* your right to relax. But the truth?

You don't have to struggle to prove you deserve success.

You don't have to be exhausted to be valuable.

The soft life is about *choosing ease where ease exists* instead of forcing things that don't align with you. It's about rejecting unnecessary stress, embracing balance, and allowing yourself to *enjoy* the life you're building instead of constantly fighting for it.

Soft Life Energy Means:

Working smarter, not harder.

- Just because something is difficult doesn't mean it's valuable. Prioritize efficiency, strategy, and systems that work for you.

Choosing opportunities that align with your well-being.

- If it costs you your peace, it's too expensive. *Not every opportunity is meant for you—and that's okay.*

Refusing to glorify overwork and exhaustion.

- You are *not* more worthy just because you're more tired. Rest is productive, too.

Moving through life with ease, not force.

- You don't have to constantly push, chase, or force things into place. *What's meant for you flows to you when you're in alignment.*

Hustle Culture Will Have You:

Feeling guilty for resting.

- As if slowing down means you're falling behind. But *rest is fuel*, not failure.

Thinking you need to "earn" relaxation.

- Newsflash: *You don't need to suffer first to deserve peace.*

Constantly feeling like you're falling behind.

- But behind *who*? Success isn't a race. Your timeline is yours.

Reminder:

Hustle culture is about proving yourself to others. The soft life is about honoring yourself.

One leads to burnout. The other leads to peace.

You get to choose.

Reflection Exercise:

- Have you ever felt guilty for resting? Why?
- How can you start embracing ease *without guilt*?

You don't have to be in a constant state of exhaustion to be worthy of success. Soft life is about working in a way that serves you—not drains you.

3. How Setting Boundaries Creates a Stress-Free Life

A soft life isn't just about what you *do*—it's about what you *no longer tolerate.*

Because let's be real: *you cannot have a peaceful life if you allow chaos to keep knocking at your door.* The more boundaries you set, the more peace you create. It's that simple.

Boundaries are the foundation of a stress-free life.

Boundaries are how you protect your energy.

Boundaries are how you stop feeling exhausted all the time.

The truth is, *people will take as much as you allow.* The more accessible you make yourself, the more people will expect from you. That's why *hard boundaries* are essential to a *soft life.*

Hard Boundaries for a Soft Life:

No to energy-draining people.

"I'm unavailable for conversations that drain my peace." If someone constantly unloads their negativity onto you, without ever offering support in return, you have every right to disengage.

No to overcommitting.

"I have too much on my plate—I can't take that on."

Stop stretching yourself thin just to please others. You are *not* required to say yes to everything.

No to burnout.

"I'm prioritizing rest without feeling guilty."

Rest isn't a luxury—it's a *necessity*. Stop treating exhaustion like a badge of honor.

No to guilt-tripping.

"My choices are mine to make—I don't owe anyone an explanation."

If someone tries to manipulate or guilt you for doing what's best for you, *remind yourself: their disappointment is not your responsibility.*

Boundaries are not about being harsh—they're about being clear.

When you respect your *own* limits, others will too. And if they don't? That's a *them* problem, not a *you* problem.

Boundaries don't push people away—they push away the stress, exhaustion, and resentment that comes from constantly overextending yourself.

Reflection Exercise:

- What's *one* area of your life where you need stronger boundaries?
- How will setting that boundary improve your peace?

A soft life is impossible without hard boundaries. The more you honor your limits, the more ease you create in your life.

4. Letting Go of Hustle Culture and Embracing Balance

We've been conditioned to think that if we're not working, we're wasting time.

But let's get one thing straight—**burnout is not a flex.**

Constant stress is not a personality trait.

And running on empty? *That's not something to be proud of.*

Somewhere along the way, we were taught that our worth is tied to how much we can *do*. That success means exhaustion. That rest is something you have to *earn* instead of something you *deserve*.

But the truth?

The goal isn't to do nothing—it's to do what actually matters.

The soft life isn't about laziness—it's about *intention*. It's about moving in alignment instead of constantly forcing things. It's about knowing that success means *nothing* if you're too drained to enjoy it.

Hustle Culture vs. Soft Life:

Hustle Culture Tells You:

- *"Sleep when you're dead."*
- *"You should always be grinding."*
- *"Resting means you're falling behind."*

Soft Life Reminds You:

- *"Rest is productive."*
- *"Alignment matters more than force."*
- *"I don't have to kill myself to succeed."*

Because *what's the point* of building a successful life if you can't even enjoy it?

How to Shift from Hustle Culture to Balance:

Prioritize joy.

Success without happiness is *pointless*. If you're not enjoying the journey, what's the rush?

Redefine productivity.

Being *productive* doesn't mean being *busy*. It means working *efficiently*—not overworking yourself into exhaustion.

Give yourself permission to slow down.

Rest is *not* a distraction from your goals—it's a necessary *part* of the process.

Reminder:

You don't have to *burn yourself out* to build a beautiful life. You don't have to *hustle 24/7* to be worthy.

You *can* thrive and *still* move with ease.

Balance isn't laziness—it's *wisdom*.

Reflection Exercise:

- What's *one* way you can shift from hustle culture to a more balanced approach in your daily life?

The more you let go of the pressure to "always be on," the more life starts to flow in your favor.

5. Respecting the Hustle – Different Paths, Same Goals

The soft life is about ease, but that doesn't mean we should dismiss or look down on people who choose the hustle. **Hustle** culture works for some people because they're in true alignment with it.

Not everyone who hustles *wins*—but the ones who do? They're not forcing it. They're not grinding just for the aesthetic or because they feel like they *have* to. **They love it, and that's why it works for them.**

And just like we don't want to be judged for choosing ease, we shouldn't judge people for choosing the grind.

The key isn't about labeling hustle culture as *good* or *bad*. The key is understanding that **everyone has their own path, and the right one is the one that aligns with who you truly are.**

Learning from Hustlers Without Losing Your Balance

Even if the hustle lifestyle isn't for you, there's *always* something to learn from those who thrive in it. Hustlers often embody traits that are valuable no matter what path you take:

Discipline. They don't wait for motivation—they show up, no matter what. Consistency is key, whether you're hustling or moving at your own pace.

Mindset. Hustlers don't just work hard—they *believe* in what they're doing. Confidence and resilience are universal success tools.

Commitment. Whether you take the hustle route or the balanced route, success requires showing up for yourself every day.

You don't have to *live* the hustle to *respect* the hustle. The goal is to appreciate different approaches while choosing the one that works best for you.

Reflection Exercise:

- Think of someone whose hustle you admire. What's one thing they do that you can apply in your own way?

The soft life and the hustle life can coexist. The key is choosing the version of success that feels right for you.

Final Thoughts: A Soft Life Requires Hard Boundaries

Living a soft life doesn't mean avoiding work—it means refusing unnecessary struggle.

Prioritizing ease isn't laziness—it's self-respect.

Protecting your peace isn't selfish—it's essential.

The key to a stress-free life? **Setting boundaries so you don't have to constantly recover from things you should've never tolerated in the first place.**

A soft life isn't just a dream—it's a *choice*. And it starts with deciding that **you are worthy of ease, balance, and peace.**

The world will always tell you to push harder, give more, and do more. But the truth? *You don't have to suffer to be successful.* You don't have to break yourself just to prove you're strong.

A soft life is possible. You just have to decide you're worthy of it.

Affirmation:

"I create a life of ease, balance, and peace. I do not glorify struggle. I set boundaries that protect my energy. I deserve a soft life."

Chapter 11: Why Privacy = Protection

Let's be real—*not everything needs to be shared.*

We live in a world that glorifies oversharing. Social media makes it seem like if you're not posting every win, every move, every relationship, or every thought, you're somehow *falling behind.* But let's pause for a second and ask:

Who is all that sharing really for?

Because here's the truth:

Some things lose their power when you put them in the wrong hands.

- *Not everyone clapping for you is happy for you.*
- *Not everyone hearing your plans wants you to succeed.*
- *Not every space is safe for your energy.*

Privacy is protection. It's not secrecy. It's not being "mysterious" for no reason. It's about **being intentional**—knowing *what* to share, *when* to share it, and *who* to share it with.

This chapter is about protecting your energy, your manifestations, and your peace by being mindful of what you allow into your space—mentally, emotionally, and physically.

Because **real self-love includes discretion.** It's about keeping some things sacred. Not because you're hiding, but because **not everything is meant for public consumption.**

1. Why Not Everything Needs to Be Shared

You don't owe the world access to your every move.

In a culture where people document every thought, every relationship, and every milestone, it's easy to feel like you *have* to share. But let's be real—not everything needs an audience.

Oversharing can feel good in the moment, but it often invites energy that you didn't ask for—opinions, doubts, jealousy, or even silent negativity. **Some things are meant to be protected, nurtured, and kept sacred until the time is right.**

When You Talk Too Soon, You Invite Outside Opinions

- Sharing your plans before they're fully formed means other people's **fears and doubts** can creep into your mind.
- People will question your vision—not because they don't believe in *you*, but because they can't see what *you* see.
- **Not everyone will understand your path, and that's okay.** Their approval isn't required.

Lesson: Speak on it **after** it's solid, not while you're still figuring it out.

When You Share Your Wins Too Openly, You Risk Attracting Envy

- Some people celebrate with you. Others feel a quiet resentment.
- Even well-meaning people can project subconscious jealousy or *why-not-me* energy onto your success.
- **Protect your accomplishments by celebrating privately first, then publicly when it feels right.**

Lesson: Enjoy the win **before** you put it on display.

When You Overshare, You Invite Unnecessary Energy Into Your Life

- Some people listen just to **gossip, judge, or compare.**
- The more people know about your life, the more they feel **entitled to have an opinion.**
- Unwanted advice, negative energy, and projections? *All side effects of oversharing.*

Lesson: **Move in silence. Let results speak louder than announcements.**

Reminder:

Not everyone needs to know what you're doing, planning, or manifesting.

Some things **grow best in private.**

Reflection Exercise:

- Think of a time you shared something too soon and felt drained or doubted afterward.
- How would you handle it differently now?

Your energy is sacred. Be selective with who gets access to it.

2. How to Cleanse Energy and Protect Your Manifestations

Your **energy is sacred.** And the things you're working on—your **dreams, goals, healing, and manifestations**—deserve *protection.*

Everything carries energy, including your intentions. When you constantly expose your manifestations to outside opinions, doubt, or negativity, **you risk disrupting their flow.** Some things are meant to be nurtured privately until they're ready to be shared.

Want your manifestations to flourish? Protect them like they're gold—because they are.

Ways to Protect Your Energy & Manifestations:
Keep your biggest moves to yourself.

- If something isn't **solid yet**, don't invite outside energy into it.
- People's doubts, fears, or negativity can **cloud your vision** before it even takes form.
- **Lesson:** *Wait until it's fully formed before you share it.*

Create a daily energy-cleansing ritual.

- Meditate to reset your mind.
- Burn sage or palo santo to clear your space.
- Take **spiritual showers** to wash away stagnant energy.
- Journal to **release negativity** and shift into alignment.
- **Lesson:** *Make cleansing a habit, not just something you do when you feel off.*

Be mindful of who you vent to.

- Some people pretend to care **just to collect information.**
- Others don't know how to hold space without projecting their fears onto you.
- **Lesson:** *Choose your safe spaces wisely.*

Protect your goals with "silent work."

- **Just because people don't see you working doesn't mean you're not making progress.**

- Some of the most powerful moves happen behind the scenes.
- **Lesson:** *Move in silence. Let results do the talking.*

Set energetic boundaries.

- Limit conversations that feel **draining**.
- Distance yourself from people who bring **drama, gossip, or doubt**.
- Pay attention to how you **feel after interacting** with certain people—your energy never lies.
- **Lesson:** *Not everyone deserves access to your space.*

Protect your physical space—don't post your home on social media.

- Your home is your sanctuary, and not everyone needs to know what it looks like.
- Posting your location, layout, or personal space **invites unnecessary energy**—and sometimes, unwanted attention.
- **Lesson:** *Keep your safe spaces sacred. Privacy is protection.*

Reminder:

Not everyone needs to have access to your **plans, energy, or dreams**. Some things grow best when they're nurtured in peace.

Keep your manifestations sacred. Protect them. Watch them flourish.

Reflection Exercise:

- What's one goal or manifestation you're working on?
- How can you protect it by keeping it sacred?

What you protect, thrives. What you expose too soon, risks interference.

3. Being Selective About What You Allow in Your Mental & Physical Space

Your space—whether it's **your mind, your home, or your social circle**—directly affects your energy.

If you've ever walked into a cluttered room and instantly felt overwhelmed, or spent time with someone who left you feeling drained, you already know this to be true. **What you allow in your space influences your peace, your focus, and your overall well-being.** That's why it's essential to be intentional about what—and who—gets access to your energy.

Mental Space:

Constantly consuming negativity, gossip, or draining conversations? It's time to detox.

Curate what you watch, read, and listen to—feed your mind with things that uplift you.

- Social media, the news, toxic group chats, certain TV shows—if it's lowering your energy, it's not worth it.
- Choose content that **inspires, educates, or genuinely entertains you** without draining you.

Physical Space:

Cluttered, chaotic environments create mental fog.

A clean, peaceful space makes you feel grounded and clear-headed.

- Your home should feel like a safe haven, not another source of stress.
- Clear out things that hold negative energy—old items, gifts from toxic people, things that no longer serve you.
- Make your space feel **intentional, peaceful, and energizing** for the life you want to live.

Social Space:
People who bring stress, gossip, or bad vibes into your life.
People who support your growth, inspire you, and bring ease.

- Be mindful of the energy people bring into your life— **are they adding to your peace or disrupting it?**
- Quality over quantity. **A small circle of uplifting, trustworthy people is worth more than a room full of fake support.**
- Distance yourself from anyone who constantly drains, manipulates, or projects negativity onto you.

Your peace is worth more than making others comfortable.

You are *not* obligated to entertain negativity, clutter, or draining relationships just because they've been part of your routine. **Be unapologetic about protecting your space—mentally, physically, and socially.**

Reflection Exercise:

- What's **one** thing you can remove from your **mental, physical, or social space** that would improve your peace?

- How can you start today?

Your environment shapes your energy. Protect it like your peace depends on it—because it does.

Final Thoughts: Your Privacy is Your Power

Keeping things sacred is a form of self-respect.

Not everyone deserves access to your personal life.

Your energy is valuable—don't waste it in spaces that don't honor it.

In a world that pushes oversharing, **privacy is a power move.** It's about protecting your peace, your manifestations, and your energy from people and spaces that don't deserve access to them.

Move in silence. Protect your peace. And remember—**not everything is meant to be shared.**

Affirmation:

"My energy, my dreams, and my peace are sacred. I move with intention. I protect my privacy because I value myself."

Part 3: Self-Love and the World Around You

Loving yourself isn't just about how you feel on the inside—it's about how you show up in the world.

Because once you truly love yourself, **everything around you shifts.**

Your environment changes. You stop tolerating toxic spaces and start creating peace.

Your mindset about success changes. You stop chasing validation and start moving with purpose.

Your relationships change. You stop proving your worth and start aligning with people who see it.

Self-love is the foundation, but it doesn't stop at you. It influences the way you interact with the world, the way you handle challenges, and the way you shape your own reality.

This section is about taking everything we've learned and **applying it to life itself.**

We're covering:

How to see every experience as an opportunity to grow.

How to break free from negative cycles and toxic influences.

The reality of success—why it's not about being "built different" but about consistency.

How to create an environment (mental, physical, and emotional) that supports your self-love journey.

This is the part where self-love **stops being a theory and becomes a lifestyle.**

It's time to **take up space, own your power, and create a life that aligns with the love you've built for yourself.**

Let's get into it.

Chapter 12: Energy Never Lies – Reading the Vibes

You ever walk into a room and *immediately* feel like something is off? Or meet someone who seems perfectly nice, but deep down, you just *don't trust their energy*?

That's not paranoia. That's **your intuition picking up on what words can't always explain.**

Energy never lies.

People can say all the right things, put on a good front, and still have **low-vibe, draining energy** that doesn't align with you. And just as important—**your own energy speaks before you do.** The way you feel, the way you carry yourself, and the way you move through life all create an energetic field that affects everything around you.

The key to **protecting your peace** is learning to **read, trust, and shift energy**—both in yourself and in others. Because when you master the ability to recognize vibes *before* they affect you, you take full control of your space, your relationships, and your well-being.

1. How to Read and Trust the Energy People Give Off

Before someone shows you who they are with their words, they show you with their energy.

You don't always need proof, a long explanation, or a list of reasons to explain why someone's vibe feels *off*. **Energy is felt before it's understood.** Your intuition picks up on shifts, micro-expressions, and unspoken signals that your conscious mind might not immediately process.

The question is—are you listening?

Signs of Low-Vibe Energy in People:
    You feel drained after talking to them.

- Their presence is emotionally exhausting, even if they don't *say* anything negative outright.

They always seem to have bad luck, drama, or chaos surrounding them.

- If every conversation revolves around negativity, gossip, or problems, *their energy is stuck in a low frequency.*

They subtly shade you but mask it as a joke.

- "Haha, I'm just playing!" But are they really? Passive-aggressive comments and backhanded compliments are signs of hidden jealousy or resentment.

They act one way around you, but different in other settings.

- If their vibe shifts depending on the audience, their energy isn't genuine.

You feel on edge or uneasy in their presence, even if nothing obvious happens.

- If your body tenses up, your stomach turns, or your mood shifts when they're around, **trust that feeling**. Your nervous system picks up on energy before your brain can rationalize it.

Signs of High-Vibe Energy in People:
    You feel lighter, inspired, or peaceful around them.

- The best connections make you feel *recharged*, not depleted.

They encourage your growth without competition or jealousy.

- They don't feel *threatened* by your wins—they celebrate them.

Their energy is consistent—you never feel like you have to guess where you stand.

- You don't have to question their intentions or worry about their loyalty.

You leave conversations feeling uplifted, not depleted.

- True high-vibe people pour into you, even in small ways. Their presence makes life feel *lighter*.

Reminder:

You **don't** need a "reason" to distance yourself from bad energy.

"I just don't like their vibe" is a valid reason.

"Something about them feels off" is a full sentence.

Your intuition is a built-in protection system—**trust it.**

Reflection Exercise:

- Think of someone in your life whose energy has always felt *off*, even if you couldn't explain why.
- Looking back, what signs were there?

Your energy is precious. Don't waste it on people who drain it.

2. Recognizing Low-Vibe vs. High-Vibe Energy in Yourself

It's easy to focus on the energy other people bring into your space, but what about the energy *you* bring?

Your own vibe is just as important as the energy you pick up from others. **The way you think, feel, and move through life shapes what you attract.** If your energy is constantly low, don't be surprised if life starts reflecting that back to you. If your energy is high, you'll notice how things start flowing effortlessly in your favor.

Everything is energy—including *you*.

High-Vibe Energy Feels Like:
Confidence and inner peace.
- You trust yourself, your decisions, and your worth—no external validation needed.

Being present in the moment, not stuck in the past or anxious about the future.
- You're not replaying old mistakes or worrying about what's next—you're *here, now*.

Gratitude, even when things aren't perfect.
- You focus on what's good instead of dwelling on what's missing.

Trusting yourself and your path.
- Even when things are uncertain, you know you're being guided in the right direction.

Low-Vibe Energy Feels Like:
Constant self-doubt, second-guessing, or seeking validation.
- You're always questioning yourself, waiting for approval, or feeling unsure of your worth.

Overthinking, fear-based decisions, or procrastination.

- You're stuck in analysis paralysis, letting fear keep you from taking action.

Feeling stuck, drained, or uninspired.

- No motivation, no excitement, just exhaustion—even from things that used to bring joy.

Allowing negativity to dictate your mood.

- Your energy shifts based on outside circumstances, instead of staying grounded in your own peace.

Your Energy Attracts What Aligns With It

Your frequency determines what (and who) shows up in your life.

If your energy is **low**, you'll attract people and situations that drain you.

If your energy is **high**, you'll naturally draw in opportunities, peace, and aligned relationships.

The question is: **What frequency are you operating on?**

Reflection Exercise:

- Reflect on a time when your energy was *high*.
- What habits, routines, or mindsets contributed to that?
- How can you recreate that feeling today?

Your energy is your responsibility. Protect it, elevate it, and watch your life shift in response.

3. Why "The Vibe is Off" is Often Your Intuition Speaking

If you've ever ignored a weird feeling and later regretted it, this is for you.

Your intuition *always* speaks to you through **energy**—the question is, are you listening?

We're conditioned to look for **logical reasons** before trusting a gut feeling, but **your intuition picks up on things your mind hasn't processed yet.** That uneasiness, that sudden shift in mood, that feeling in your body that you can't quite explain? **It's real.**

That "something's off" feeling? Trust it.

That tension in your stomach when you're around certain people? That's a sign.

That instant relief when someone leaves your space? Your body knows what your mind won't admit.

Your **nervous system** picks up on energy shifts *before* your brain can put words to them. That's why you can feel weird around someone even if they've "never done anything wrong." It's not paranoia—it's **awareness.**

How to Strengthen Your Intuition About Energy:

Pay attention to patterns.

- If someone always leaves you feeling **exhausted, anxious, or uneasy**, that's not random.
- One bad day is a coincidence. A *pattern* means something deeper is off.

Notice how you feel after interactions.

- Do you feel **lighter, inspired, and peaceful** after being with them?
- Or do you feel **drained, irritable, or off-balance?**

- *Your energy after the interaction tells you everything you need to know.*

Stop gaslighting yourself.
- If your gut tells you something isn't right, **trust that feeling.**
- You don't need proof. You don't need to explain it to anyone.
- **Your intuition doesn't require other people's validation.**

Energy Doesn't Lie, But People Do.

If something feels **off**, it *is.*

If someone's energy shifts, **believe it before they even say a word.**

If your body reacts before your mind understands, **don't brush it off.**

Your intuition is your built-in **protection system**—it will never steer you wrong.

Reflection Exercise:
- Think of a time your **gut feeling** about someone was *right.*
- What signs were there?
- How can you start trusting your intuition *more* moving forward?

The more you trust your intuition, the stronger it becomes. Listen to it—it's speaking for a reason.

4. How to Shift Your Energy and Protect It from Negativity

Protecting your energy is an act of self-love. If something feels heavy, draining, or misaligned, **you have the power to shift it.**

You don't have to stay in spaces that deplete you. You don't have to entertain conversations that lower your frequency. **Your energy is yours to protect, and no one else is going to do it for you.**

The best part? *Energy is fluid.* Just like you can absorb negativity, you can also **release it and shift back into alignment.**

Ways to Protect & Shift Your Energy:
Limit access.

- *Not everyone deserves a front-row seat to your life.*
- Be selective about who and what you allow into your space.

Energetic cleansing.

- Sage, palo santo, meditation, journaling, spiritual baths—find what helps you reset.
- Energy lingers, so clearing it regularly keeps your space and mind clear.

Mindful consumption.

- *The music, social media, and conversations you engage with affect your vibration.*
- Ask yourself: **Is this content feeding me, or is it draining me?**

Set energetic boundaries.

- If a space or situation **drains you**, remove yourself from it—*no explanation needed.*
- Your peace is not up for debate.

Spend time in high-vibe environments.

- Nature, music, deep conversations, movement—*these all raise your frequency.*
- Surround yourself with **people, places, and practices** that make you feel **light, inspired, and aligned.**

Your Energy is Your Responsibility.

No one else will protect it for you.

If it drains you, distance yourself from it.

If it lifts you, pour more into it.

Your energy shapes your reality—so guard it like your life depends on it.

Because **it does.**

Reflection Exercise:

- What's *one* thing in your life that **consistently lowers your energy**?
- How can you start limiting its influence?
- What **habit** can you build to protect your energy daily?

Energy flows where attention goes—make sure yours is going in the right direction.

Final Thoughts: Energy Speaks Louder Than Words

Energy doesn't lie. If something feels off, it probably is.

Your energy is magnetic—keep it high, and watch what shifts.

Protecting your peace isn't rude, it's self-respect.

The more you **trust, read, and protect energy**, the more aligned and peaceful your life will become. **Your vibe sets the tone for everything around you—honor it, protect it, and move accordingly.**

Affirmation:

"I trust my intuition. I attract high-vibe people and situations. I release anything that disrupts my peace."

Chapter 13: Unsubscribe from the BS

Let's be honest—**not everything deserves your energy.**

You don't need to engage in every argument.

You don't need to entertain every toxic situation.

You don't need to explain yourself to people committed to misunderstanding you.

Because here's the truth: **every interaction is an exchange of energy.** And the more you engage in negativity, the more you allow it to drain you. Not everything is worth your time, not every comment needs a clapback, and not every situation deserves your presence.

Not everything needs a response. Some things just need distance.

Unsubscribing from the BS isn't about being passive—it's about being **intentional**. It's knowing when to disengage, when to let go, and when to choose *peace over pettiness.*

This chapter is about **cutting toxic cycles, stepping back from unnecessary drama, and mastering the art of detachment.** Because *real self-love?* **It's knowing when to walk away—and never looking back.**

1. How to Identify and Cut Off Toxic Cycles

Toxic cycles feel familiar, but that doesn't mean they're healthy.

Toxic cycles aren't random—they're **patterns** that repeat over and over. Same situation, different day. You tell yourself *this time will* *be different*, but somehow, you end up back in the same emotional mess.

Most of the time, toxic cycles are fueled by **guilt, obligation, or fear.** You don't stay because it's good for you—you stay because a part of you feels like you *have to.* But here's the thing:

The only way to break a toxic cycle is to stop participating in it.

Let's identify the signs that you're stuck in a loop that's not serving you.

Signs You're Stuck in a Toxic Cycle:
Same problem, different person.
- You keep attracting the same kind of toxic relationships, friendships, or work situations. Different names, different faces, **same red flags.**

Walking on eggshells.
- You constantly **filter yourself** to avoid triggering someone's reactions. You hold back your opinions, shrink yourself, or change your behavior just to **keep the peace.**

Emotional whiplash.
- One day, things are great. The next, it's chaos. You never know what to expect, and the **instability keeps you hooked.** It's like a rollercoaster you *didn't* sign up for, but you keep riding anyway.

You feel drained but obligated.

- You know the situation is bad for you, but something keeps pulling you back—**guilt, fear of being alone, or the hope that things will change.**

The Question That Will Set You Free:

If nothing changed about this situation, would I still want to be in it?

Sit with that. Because if the answer is *no*, then it's time to stop waiting for change that will never come. **Your peace isn't worth the cycle.**

Reflection Exercise:
- Think of a **toxic cycle** you've been in.
- What kept you **stuck**? Was it guilt, fear, obligation, or something else?
- What would it look like to fully **walk away**?

Breaking the cycle isn't easy, but staying in it is harder. Choose yourself.

2. Learning to Disengage from Drama Without Feeling Guilty

Not every problem is yours to fix.

Some people *thrive* on drama. They **love** chaos. They *need* an audience. And if you're not careful, they'll pull you into their mess just to keep the show going.

But here's the truth: **You don't have to be part of the performance.**

Walking away from drama isn't avoidance—it's self-respect.

You don't need to **defend yourself** in every situation. You don't need to **prove your point** to people committed to misunderstanding you. You don't need to **explain your choices** to people who *live* for gossip.

The most powerful move? **Disengaging completely.**

How to Exit Drama Without Guilt:
Recognize the bait.

- Some people will **say wild things** just to get a reaction.
- They'll poke, provoke, and push until you snap—**don't take the bait.**
- If someone wants to argue just for the sake of arguing, let them argue *with themselves.*

Be okay with being misunderstood.

- Not everyone **deserves** an explanation.
- Let them think what they want. Their opinion of you is **none of your business.**

Redirect the conversation.

- If someone starts **gossiping or dragging you into mess,** shut it down.
- A simple, *"I'm focused on more positive things right now"* sets the tone.
- If they keep pushing? That's your sign to **create more distance.**

Create distance.

- If someone's **energy is always chaotic,** stop giving them **so much access** to you.

- Protect your peace **like it's your most valuable asset—because it is.**

Reminder:
Not engaging isn't weakness—it's wisdom.
Silence is often the loudest response.
If it doesn't bring you peace, let it go.

Reflection Exercise:
- What's a situation where you got pulled into drama you didn't need to be in?
- How could you handle it differently next time?

The more you disengage from the BS, the more peaceful your life becomes.

3. Why Not Every Argument Needs a Response (Silence is Power)

Some battles aren't worth fighting.

Let's be real—**not everyone arguing with you actually wants resolution.** Some people argue just to get a reaction. Some argue because they *thrive* in negativity. And some argue just to feel like they have power over you.

But here's the truth:

You do not have to correct every false narrative about you.
You do not have to match someone's negative energy.
You do not have to win every argument.
Silence is power.

You don't need to defend yourself against people who are *committed* to misunderstanding you. You don't need to waste your breath proving your worth to someone who doesn't respect you. And you definitely don't need to meet low-vibe energy with more low-vibe energy.

Sometimes, the most powerful response? **No response at all.**

When People Try to Provoke You:
Let them talk.
Your energy is too expensive to spend on cheap drama.

When People Try to Drag You Into Negativity:
Let them stay there.
You don't have to go where you weren't invited.

When People Expect a Reaction:
Give them none.
Your silence forces them to deal with themselves.

What Silence Does for You:
It removes your energy from the situation.
- The moment you stop feeding negativity, it stops having power over you.

It forces the other person to deal with themselves.
- Without your reaction, they're left arguing with *themselves.*

It keeps your peace intact.

- No drained energy, no wasted words, no unnecessary stress.

You Don't Win by Proving a Point—You Win by Protecting Your Peace.

Your silence doesn't mean they're right.

Your silence doesn't mean you lost.

Your silence means **you refuse to let negativity control you.**

Reflection Exercise:

- Think of a time when you engaged in an unnecessary argument.
- How would *silence* have served you better?

Not every battle is yours to fight. Choose your peace over proving a point.

4. Mastering the Art of Peace > Pettiness

Let's be real—**pettiness is tempting.**

We've *all* had those moments where we wanted to clap back, prove a point, or remind someone that they had us *all the way* messed up. And let's be honest—sometimes, it feels **good** in the moment.

But the truth?

Pettiness only satisfies you for a moment. Peace satisfies you for life.

Clapping back **doesn't fix anything**—it just keeps you engaged in a cycle that drains you. And for what? To prove something to people who don't even matter in the bigger picture?

Choosing peace isn't about letting people slide—it's about letting yourself rise.

How to Choose Peace Over Pettiness:
Remember your power.
- Being *unbothered* is the ultimate flex.
- They want a reaction? *Don't give them one.*

Ask yourself: Will this matter in a month?
- If the answer is *no*, let it go.
- Don't waste your energy on things that won't even cross your mind later.

Walk away from low-vibe energy.
- You don't need to **prove anything** to people operating from negativity.
- The moment you disengage, they lose their power over you.

Let karma do its job.
- What people put out **comes back to them**—good or bad.
- You don't have to deliver the lesson. Life will.

The Most Powerful Move You Can Make? Choosing Peace Every Single Time.

Your energy is *too valuable* to waste on temporary satisfaction.

Let them talk. Let them assume. Let them be messy. Your peace is **worth more** than their validation.

Reflection Exercise:

- When was the last time you felt **tempted to be petty**?
- What would *choosing peace* have looked like instead?

Petty is a moment. Peace is a lifestyle. Choose wisely.

Final Thoughts: Your Energy is Too Valuable for BS

Not everything needs a reaction.

Not everyone deserves a response.

Not every situation requires your energy.

Your **peace is too expensive** to be wasted on nonsense. The more you protect it, the more your life flows in alignment.

If something **doesn't serve you, unsubscribe.** No guilt, no explanation—just peace.

Affirmation:

"I protect my energy. I do not entertain drama. My peace is my priority, and I choose it every time."

Chapter 14: Trust Your Gut – Strengthening Your Intuition

Your **intuition** is your **built-in guidance system.** It's always there, always speaking to you—**but are you listening?**

You've probably had moments where you just *knew* something wasn't right, even if you couldn't explain why. Or maybe you've felt an instant connection with someone *before* they even said a word.

That's intuition.

It's not magic. It's not guesswork. It's a mix of **subconscious knowledge, inner wisdom, and self-trust.** Your intuition picks up on energy, patterns, and unspoken details *before your mind fully processes them.*

But in a world that constantly tells you to **doubt yourself,** trusting your gut can feel difficult.

This chapter is about:

Strengthening your intuition so it becomes second nature.

Learning the difference between fear and instinct.

Reconnecting with your inner voice so you stop second-guessing yourself.

Because when you **trust your gut?** *You move differently.*

1. What Intuition Really Is

Intuition is your brain making connections faster than you can logically process them.

It's not magic. It's not just a "feeling." It's your mind, body, and subconscious working together—pulling from past experiences, picking up on energy shifts, and analyzing patterns *before* your rational mind catches up.

Think about how a skilled musician can hear a note and immediately know if it's out of tune, or how an experienced driver can sense danger on the road before it happens. That's intuition— **rapid, subconscious processing based on everything you've observed and experienced.**

Your gut feeling is the result of all that **information coming together in an instant.**

Why Intuition Feels Like a Sixth Sense

Your mind is always picking up on things you're not consciously aware of.

- The micro-expressions on someone's face.
- The slight change in their tone.
- The shift in energy when you walk into a room.

All of these small details add up, sending signals to your nervous system before your mind can fully process *why* something feels off— or perfectly right.

Intuition often speaks through the body before the mind.

- A tight stomach when something feels wrong.
- Goosebumps when something feels eerily accurate.
- A sudden sense of relief when you make the right decision.

Your body **reacts first**—your logical mind catches up later.

Your subconscious stores patterns and lessons, even when you don't realize it.

- That's why you might feel uneasy about someone **before** they even do anything wrong. Your mind has picked up on familiar behaviors from past experiences.
- Or why you instantly click with certain people—it's not random. Your energy recognizes something safe, familiar, or aligned with you.

Everyday Examples of Intuition at Work

You can sense when someone is lying—even if their words sound convincing.

You feel uneasy before walking into a situation that turns out to be bad.

You just know when something is right for you—even if it doesn't make logical sense yet.

You think of someone, and they randomly call or text you.

You get a gut feeling to take a different route home—only to find out there was a major accident on your usual path.

Your intuition is **always working.**

The question is—**are you listening?**

Reflection Exercise:

- Think of a time you *just knew* something before you had proof.
- What did your intuition tell you?
- Were you right?

The more you trust your intuition, the sharper it becomes.

2. The Difference Between Intuition and Fear

Not every gut feeling is intuition. Sometimes, it's just **anxiety in disguise.**

Your mind can play tricks on you. It can replay past experiences, amplify self-doubt, and make you second-guess everything. **Your intuition, on the other hand, is clear, calm, and direct.**

The problem? Fear can *feel* like intuition if you don't know how to tell them apart. Fear speaks in worst-case scenarios. Intuition speaks in *certainty.* Fear is loud, frantic, and desperate. Intuition is quiet, steady, and unwavering.

How to Tell the Difference Between Intuition and Fear:

Intuition feels grounded.

- It's a quiet but strong **knowing**—you don't have to overthink it.
- It doesn't come from overanalyzing or second-guessing—it's just *there.*
- Even if it doesn't make logical sense yet, it feels **stable and sure.**
- **Example:** You meet someone and **instantly feel safe**— or **instantly feel off.**

Fear feels anxious and loud.

- It's full of **doubt, hesitation, and worst-case scenarios.**
- It's based on **past trauma or insecurities**, not the present moment.
- It leads to **overthinking, procrastination, and avoidance.**

- **Example:** You hesitate to take a new opportunity, not because it's wrong, but because you're **afraid of failing.**

How to Strengthen the Connection to Your Intuition

Check your body's reaction.

- Intuition often shows up as **a calm certainty, a gut feeling, or a knowing deep in your bones.**
- Fear tends to show up as **racing thoughts, shallow breathing, or tightness in your chest.**

Ask yourself: Am I feeling this because of past wounds or present truth?

- If the feeling is coming from old trauma or self-doubt, **it's fear.**
- If the feeling is coming from the present moment and has no emotional charge, **it's intuition.**

Slow down before reacting.

- Fear demands **instant decisions** based on panic.
- Intuition gives you space and clarity—even if it's urgent, it won't feel rushed.

Trust and test it.

- Start noticing the times your **intuition was right** versus the times fear held you back.
- The more you trust it, the stronger it gets.

Intuition Protects You. Fear Limits You.

When you learn to tell the difference, you stop doubting yourself and start making **aligned choices.**

Reflection Exercise:

- Think of a decision you've avoided out of fear.
- Was it **true intuition** warning you away from something bad?
- Or was it **self-doubt** holding you back from something good?

Your intuition already knows the answer. You just have to trust it.

3. Why People Feel Disconnected from Their Intuition

If **intuition is natural**, why do so many people struggle to trust it?

Because modern life is designed to disconnect you from yourself.

From the moment you wake up, your mind is bombarded with **outside influences**—social media, news, opinions, expectations, and endless distractions. In a world that constantly tells you what to think, how to feel, and what to do, **it's easy to lose touch with your inner voice.**

Reasons People Feel Disconnected from Their Intuition:

Overstimulation – Constant noise drowns out your inner voice.

- Social media, notifications, and endless scrolling **keep your brain distracted 24/7.**
- When you're constantly consuming **outside input**, there's no **quiet space** to hear your own instincts.
- You start **reacting** to everything instead of truly *feeling* what's right for you.

Self-Doubt – You've been conditioned to trust outside opinions more than your own.

- Since childhood, you've been taught to **listen to authority figures, experts, and rules**—which can make you question your own instincts.

- You hesitate because you fear being **wrong, irrational, or judged.**

- You might even **gaslight yourself**—thinking, *Maybe I'm overreacting. Maybe I'm imagining things.*

People-Pleasing – You ignore your gut to keep others happy.

- You feel a **gut reaction** telling you to walk away, but you stay because you don't want to upset anyone.

- You **put others' comfort above your own truth**, even when it drains you.

- The more you **ignore** your gut, the weaker your connection to it becomes.

Over-Reliance on Logic – Trying to "prove" what you feel.

- Intuition doesn't always have **immediate proof**—but logic demands evidence.

- If something feels off, your mind starts overanalyzing instead of just *trusting* the feeling.

- You hesitate, rationalize, or talk yourself out of your first instinct.

The more you **override, ignore, or second-guess** your gut, the harder it becomes to recognize. **But it's always there—waiting for you to listen.**

Reminder:

Your intuition **never disappeared**—it's just buried under **noise, self-doubt, and external conditioning.**

If you feel disconnected from your inner voice, know this: **You can always return to it.** The next step? Learning how to *reconnect* and strengthen it.

Reflection Exercise:

- What's one habit or influence in your life that **distracts** you from your intuition?
- Have you ever **ignored your gut feeling** and later regretted it?

Your intuition is like a muscle—the more you use it, the stronger it gets.

4. Ways to Reconnect with Your Intuition

Your intuition **never left you**—it just got buried under distractions, self-doubt, and outside noise. **Reconnecting with it is about quieting the chaos and learning to trust yourself again.**

The more you listen, the stronger it gets. Here's how to start:

Practice Stillness

Your intuition speaks in silence, not noise.

- If your mind is always busy, you won't hear your inner voice.
- Meditation, mindfulness, or even just sitting quietly for a few minutes a day helps you tune in.

- Go for a walk without your phone, turn off distractions, and just **be present**—your intuition will come through.

Notice Patterns in Feelings & Experiences

Your intuition has been guiding you all along—have you noticed the patterns?

- Have you ignored red flags in the past, only to regret it later?
- Do you keep attracting the same type of people or situations?
- If the same feelings keep showing up, your intuition is **trying to tell you something.**

Example: If every time you ignore your gut about someone, it turns out they weren't good for you, **that's a sign to start listening sooner.**

Pay Attention to Your Body's Reactions

Your body reacts before your mind catches up.

- Ever feel **tightness, knots, or discomfort** around certain people or decisions? *That's usually a warning.*
- Ever feel **light, open, or excited** about something—even if it doesn't make logical sense? *That's a green flag.*

Your body **knows the truth before your mind processes it.** Learn to read the signs.

Ask Yourself Direct Questions

Instead of overthinking, simplify it.

- Ask yourself: **"Does this feel right?"**

- Trust your **first instinct**—before your mind starts analyzing and second-guessing.
- If you feel **at peace with a choice**, it's likely your intuition. If you feel **uneasy**, listen to that too.

Avoid External Validation as a Crutch

The more you rely on others for answers, the weaker your intuition becomes.

- Do you always ask for advice before making a decision?
- Do you second-guess yourself because you want reassurance?

Try making **small decisions on your own**—like what to eat, what to wear, or what route to take—**without asking for input.** This builds confidence in your ability to **trust yourself.**

Intuition is Like a Muscle—The More You Use It, The Stronger It Gets.

At first, you might feel uncertain. That's normal. But over time, you'll realize **your gut has always known what's best for you.**

Reflection Exercise:

- Try a **24-hour period** of making decisions **without asking anyone else for advice.**
- Notice how it feels. Were your instincts right? Did you feel more in control?

Your intuition is your superpower—start using it.

5. Strengthening Your Intuition – Practical Exercises

Your intuition is like a muscle—the more you use it, the stronger it gets. The goal is to start recognizing **how** your gut speaks to you and build trust in your own inner guidance. Here are three practical ways to sharpen your intuition:

Journal Prompt: Recall a Time Your Intuition Was Right

Reflect on a time when you had a gut feeling about something—and you were right.

- **What happened?**
- **How did your body react before you realized the truth?** (Did you feel tense, calm, excited, uneasy?)
- **Did you listen to your intuition right away, or did you ignore it at first?**
- **How can you trust yourself more moving forward?**

Recognizing past intuitive moments helps you see how accurate your gut already is.

The "Gut Check" Practice for Decisions

Next time you need to make a decision—big or small:

1. **Sit in silence** and ask yourself: *Does this feel right?*
2. Notice your **first reaction**—before doubt or overthinking kicks in.
3. **Pay attention to the physical feeling:**
   - If it feels **light, exciting, or peaceful**, that's usually a yes.
   - If it feels **heavy, tight, or uncertain**, that's usually a no.

4.   Follow through **without second-guessing.**

This exercise helps you learn how intuition speaks through feelings instead of logic.

A 7-Day Intuition Challenge

For the next 7 days, challenge yourself to rely on your **intuition over external opinions.**

Each morning, ask yourself: *What do I need today? (More rest? A change of routine? A creative outlet?)* Follow your first instinct.

Make one small decision each day without overthinking. Start with simple choices—what to eat, what music to listen to, which direction to walk.

Pay attention to your body's reactions in conversations, relationships, and situations. Who makes you feel at ease? Who makes you feel tense?

Reflect on intuitive moments at the end of each day. Write down anything that felt like a gut instinct—did it turn out to be right?

The more you listen to your intuition, the clearer it becomes.

Final Thoughts: Your Intuition is Your Superpower

Your intuition is always speaking—your job is to listen.

The more you trust it, the stronger it gets.

You already have all the answers inside you. Stop looking outside for what's always been within.

Your intuition has been guiding you all along. Every time you second-guess yourself, overanalyze a decision, or seek external validation, you're just delaying what you *already know to be true.*

The real flex? **Trusting yourself so deeply that you no longer need confirmation.**

The more you listen, the more aligned your life becomes. **Your intuition is your superpower—use it.**

Affirmation:

"I trust myself. My intuition is strong. I always know what's right for me."

Chapter 15: The Reality of Success – "You Are Not Built Different"

Let's get something straight—**successful people are not magical, superhuman beings.**

They don't have some secret genetic advantage.

They don't wake up with unlimited motivation every day.

They're not built *any different* than you.

The only difference? They made a decision to be **consistent.**

We love to believe success is about **luck, talent, or special circumstances**—because it gives us an excuse. It's easier to think that successful people have *something we don't* rather than admit that the real difference is **effort, consistency, and mindset.**

Here's the reality:

Successful people aren't always motivated—but they still show up.

They don't have perfect conditions—they just work with what they have.

They don't wait for inspiration—they create habits that keep them moving.

Success isn't about waiting for the perfect moment. It's about moving forward, even when it's uncomfortable, even when it's inconvenient, even when no one is watching.

This chapter is about stripping away the illusions around success and breaking it down to what it *really* is:

Mindset + Consistency + Effort.

Small steps, repeated over time.

Paying the cost of success—and understanding why it's worth it.

Because when you realize that **no one is "built different"**, you stop making excuses and start **building the life you actually want.**

1. Successful People Are Just People – Mindset is the Key

The biggest lie people believe about success:

"They must have something I don't."

You see successful people and assume they were always confident, always knew what they were doing, always had some special advantage. But here's the truth:

They doubted themselves.

They failed.

They wanted to quit.

They didn't feel like doing the work some days.

The only reason they succeeded? *They didn't stop.*

Success isn't about talent, luck, or even intelligence—it's about **how you think and how you move forward, even when it's hard.**

The Mindset Shift That Changes Everything

Instead of thinking: *"I'm not built like that."*

Start thinking: *"I can learn, adapt, and improve."*

Instead of thinking: *"I don't have the motivation."*

Start thinking: *"I don't need motivation. I need discipline."*

Instead of thinking: *"I don't know where to start."*

Start thinking: *"I'll start small and figure it out along the way."*

The way you think about success determines whether or not you achieve it.

People who succeed aren't *different* from you—they just think differently. They reframe excuses into challenges, and challenges into opportunities.

Reflection Exercise:
- Write down **one excuse** you've told yourself about why you *can't* succeed.
- Now **reframe it** into a truth that empowers you.

Your success starts with your mindset. Change that, and you change everything.

2. "Where There's a Will, There's a Way" – Small Steps Create Big Results

You don't need to have it all figured out. You just need to start.

Too many people get stuck **waiting**—waiting for the perfect moment, the perfect plan, or the perfect conditions. They want a **guarantee** that it will work out before they even take action.

But here's the truth: **The way is created by walking it.**

No one successful had the whole path mapped out from the beginning. They started **before they felt ready** and figured things out along the way. **You don't need certainty—you just need movement.**

How to Start Small and Build Momentum
Pick one goal.

- Don't try to change your whole life at once—just focus on *one* thing.
- Success is built step by step, not all at once.

Break it into tiny steps.

- Ask yourself: *What's the smallest possible action I can take today?*
- If your goal feels overwhelming, **make it smaller** until it feels doable.

Build consistency over intensity.

- **Small daily actions beat big occasional efforts.**
- Doing something **every day for 5 minutes** is better than doing something **for 2 hours once a month.**

Track your progress.

- Even **small wins add up**—seeing them helps keep you motivated.
- Keep a simple log, journal, or checklist to remind yourself **how far you've come.**

Success is a Daily Habit, Not a One-Time Event

- **Want to be healthier?** Walk for **10 minutes today.**
- **Want to start a business?** Spend **15 minutes researching today.**
- **Want to write a book?** Write **200 words today.**

The goal is not perfection—it's momentum.

You don't need to do *everything* today. You just need to do *something.*

Reflection Exercise:

- What's one goal you've been putting off because it "feels too big"?
- What's one small step you can take today to start?

Your dream isn't out of reach—you just haven't taken the first step yet.

3. The Cost of Success – Time, Energy, Effort (And Why It's Worth It)

Success is expensive, but so is regret.

Here's the truth most people don't want to hear: **Success costs something.**

It costs time.

It costs energy.

It costs discipline.

It costs stepping outside of your comfort zone.

And if you're not willing to **pay that price?** You stay exactly where you are.

The Question You Need to Ask Yourself:

"Am I willing to trade short-term comfort for long-term success?"

Because **staying the same has a cost too.**

The Cost of Staying the Same:

- Waking up **10 years from now** wishing you had started.
- Watching **other people live the life you wanted** while you're still stuck in place.

- Knowing you **could've done more—but didn't.**

The truth? **You're paying a price either way.**

Choose your hard. The discomfort of growth is **temporary—** the pain of regret **lasts forever.**

Why It's Worth It

Success isn't just about money, status, or external rewards. It's about **becoming who you were meant to be.**

Proving to yourself that you can do it.

- The moment you push past your limits, you start seeing what you're truly capable of.

Living life on your own terms.

- Freedom comes when you take control of your future.

Becoming the best version of yourself.

- Growth isn't easy, but staying stagnant feels even worse.

The **price of success** is **effort.** The **reward?** A life that actually fulfills you.

Reflection Exercise:

- **What's one "cost" of success that has held you back?** (Time? Effort? Fear of failure?)
- **How can you shift your mindset to see it as an investment in yourself instead?**

The price of success is temporary. The regret of never trying? That's forever.

Final Thoughts: No One is Built Different—They Just Didn't Quit

Success isn't about being special. It's about being consistent.

Small steps every day will take you further than waiting for the "right" moment.

The price of success is high—but the price of regret is higher.

You don't need to be *more talented, more gifted, or more "built for this"* than anyone else. The only thing separating you from success is **whether or not you keep going.**

So the real question is: **Are you ready to stop making excuses and start making moves?**

Affirmation:

"I am capable of success. I take small steps daily. I create my own opportunities. I am not waiting—I am building."

Chapter 16: Secure the Bag… and Your Self-Worth

Let's be real—**self-worth is the real flex.**

It's not about:

How much money you make.

How many people like you.

How "impressive" your life looks on the outside.

Proving anything to anyone.

True security comes from knowing your worth—without needing external validation to confirm it.

When you move from **self-worth instead of scarcity,** *everything shifts.*

You make better choices. You stop settling for jobs, relationships, or situations that don't serve you.

You attract better relationships. You don't chase, you align. People who value you **match your energy.**

You level up your entire life. When you believe you deserve better, you start making decisions that reflect that belief.

Because here's the truth: **Money is important, but self-respect is priceless.**

There's nothing wrong with wanting financial success. **Securing the bag is a must.** But **how** you secure it *matters.* If you're compromising your dignity, overworking to prove your value, or chasing approval from others—**the bag is securing you, not the other way around.**

This chapter is about **securing the bag—financially, emotionally, and mentally—without sacrificing your dignity or chasing things that don't align with your value.**

Because the biggest power move? Knowing that YOU are the prize.

When you start treating yourself like one, **the world has no choice but to follow suit.**

1. Why Self-Worth is the Real Flex

People who know their worth don't settle for crumbs.

They don't **chase, beg,** or **lower their standards** just to be chosen—whether it's in **relationships, friendships, or business.** They move with confidence, not desperation.

When you truly know your worth, you stop entertaining anything that doesn't align with it.

What Moving from Self-Worth Looks Like:

You make choices based on what aligns with you, not what you think will impress others.

- You don't say *yes* to opportunities just because they look good on paper.
- You prioritize what **feels right** over what looks good to others.

You don't over-explain yourself—your value speaks for itself.

- You don't waste time **convincing people** to respect you.
- You let your **actions, mindset, and presence** do the talking.

You don't seek validation—you already know who you are.

- You don't need likes, approval, or external validation to feel valuable.
- You trust yourself first, always.

You walk away when something doesn't serve you, instead of staying out of fear.

- You don't stay in situations just because they're **comfortable** or because you're afraid of being alone.
- You know that anything you lose by choosing yourself **wasn't meant for you anyway.**

Reminder: The moment you realize your value, the game changes.

When you move from a place of **self-worth, confidence, and alignment**, life starts reflecting that back to you. You start attracting people, opportunities, and experiences that match your energy—because you no longer tolerate anything less.

Reflection Exercise:

- **Think of a time you accepted less than you deserved.**
- **What would you do differently now, knowing your worth?**

Self-worth isn't just something you think—it's something you live.

2. How to Make Choices from Abundance, Not Desperation

Desperation leads to bad decisions.

When you operate from a **scarcity mindset**, you make choices out of **fear instead of alignment.** You cling to things that don't serve you because you're afraid you won't find something better.

- **Taking jobs that drain you** because you're scared you won't find better.
- **Staying in relationships that don't fulfill you** because you're afraid of being alone.
- **Saying "yes" to things that don't align** because you think you won't get another opportunity.

Scarcity mindset says:

"I better take what I can get."

"If I don't accept this, I might never get another chance."

"I have to prove my worth to be chosen."

Scarcity makes you **grasp, settle, and shrink** yourself just to keep things that aren't even good for you.

What an Abundance Mindset Looks Like:

"What's meant for me will not miss me."

- You trust that the right opportunities, people, and situations will come—so you don't have to chase.

"If this isn't right for me, something better is coming."

- Instead of clinging to what's not working, you release it and stay open to what's next.

"I don't chase, I attract."

- You align your energy with what you want, instead of desperately running after things that aren't for you.

When you move from **abundance**, you make **choices that align with your future—not your fears.**

Reflection Exercise:

- Think of a time you made a choice from scarcity.
- What would choosing from abundance have looked like instead?

The world mirrors how you see yourself. When you believe in your worth, life will start reflecting that belief back to you.

3. Avoiding Pick-Me Energy in Relationships, Work, and Friendships

Pick-me energy is rooted in low self-worth.

It's when you feel like you have to **compete** for attention, approval, or validation—whether it's in **relationships, friendships, or even your career.** Instead of standing in your worth, you overextend yourself, hoping to be *chosen.*

But here's the truth: The people, jobs, and relationships meant for you will never require you to **beg, prove, or overcompensate.**

Examples of Pick-Me Energy:

In Relationships:

- Overgiving without receiving the same effort in return.
- Tolerating disrespect, inconsistency, or emotional unavailability just to "keep" someone.
- Trying to **"prove" you're different** from others, as if your value needs validation.

At Work:

- Overworking, **taking on too much**, or **underpricing** your skills just to be seen as valuable.

- Thinking you have to **"earn" basic respect** instead of recognizing your worth from the start.
- Staying in toxic workplaces because you don't believe you can find something better.

In Friendships:
- Being the **only one** putting in effort, making plans, or checking in.
- Accepting **one-sided relationships** where you're always giving but rarely receiving.
- Shrinking yourself to be more *likable* instead of **being your full self.**

How to Avoid Pick-Me Energy:

Know you are the prize.
- You don't have to **prove** your worth—it's already there.
- The right people, opportunities, and relationships will **recognize your value without you having to beg.**

Stop over-explaining.
- People who truly value you **won't need convincing.**
- The more you try to justify your worth, the more you attract people who don't see it.

Match energy, don't chase it.
- If someone isn't meeting you **halfway**, stop overextending yourself.

- The right people will **reciprocate effortlessly**—you won't have to fight for their attention or respect.

Know that rejection is redirection.
- If something doesn't work out, **it wasn't for you.**
- The universe removes things that don't align to make space for **what actually does.**

Reminder:
The **right opportunities, relationships, and friendships** will choose you **without you having to beg for them.**
If you have to **chase, force, or prove** your worth—it's not for you.

Reflection Exercise:
- **Where in your life have you been operating from a "pick-me" mentality?**
- **How can you shift into knowing you are the prize?**

When you fully embrace your worth, everything that isn't aligned with it naturally falls away.

4. Why Leveling Up Your Mindset Levels Up Your Life
Your life reflects your mindset. Period.

If you believe you're unworthy, you'll tolerate less than you deserve.
If you think money is scarce, you'll stay in jobs that drain you.
If you think love is rare, you'll accept relationships that don't fulfill you.

But when you change your mindset? Your life follows.

Your thoughts shape your choices. Your choices shape your habits. And your habits shape your reality. If you want to **level up your life, you have to start with your mindset.**

How to Shift Into a High-Value Mindset:

Stop thinking small.

- If someone else can do it, **so can you.**
- The only difference between you and successful people? **They believe they can.**

Release survival mode.

- You weren't born just to work, struggle, and repeat. **You deserve to live, not just survive.**
- Operating from **scarcity and fear** keeps you stuck— abundance starts with *believing* you are worthy of more.

Expect better for yourself.

- High standards are not "too much"—they're a **filter** for the right people and opportunities.
- Stop settling for *just okay* when **great is out there.**

Invest in yourself.

- The best return you'll ever get is **on what you put into YOU.**
- Whether it's education, self-care, new skills, or mindset work—**what you invest in yourself will always pay off.**

When You Elevate Your Mindset, You Elevate Your Reality.

The way you think affects **everything**. If you shift your beliefs, your actions will follow—and so will your results.

Reflection Exercise:

- **What's one limiting belief about yourself that's been keeping you stuck?**
- **How can you reframe it into a belief that empowers you?**

Your mind is the foundation of your success. Upgrade it, and everything else will follow.

Final Thoughts: Secure the Bag... and Your Worth

Your self-worth dictates everything—your money, your relationships, your opportunities.

When you move from abundance, life flows.

You don't need to prove yourself—your value speaks for itself.

When you truly know your worth, **you stop begging, chasing, or settling.** You make moves with confidence, knowing that what's meant for you will align without force.

So the real question is: *Are you moving like someone who knows their worth?*

Affirmation:

"I move from self-worth, not desperation. I make choices that align with my value. I do not chase—I attract what is meant for me."

Chapter 17: Making Your Environment Work for You

Your environment isn't just **where you live**—it's the **energy you surround yourself with.**

It's the **people** in your life.

It's the **places** you spend time in.

It's the **content** you consume.

It's the **thoughts** you allow in your mind.

Your environment either supports your growth or holds you back.

The right space? It makes you feel **safe, inspired, and aligned.** **The wrong space?** It keeps you **stuck in cycles that don't serve you.**

You can have **all the ambition in the world**, but if your environment is draining, negative, or uninspiring, it will slow you down. The people you surround yourself with, the conversations you engage in, and even the clutter in your space **affect your mindset and energy.**

This chapter is about creating an environment—**physically, mentally, and emotionally**—that supports your **self-love, success, and well-being.**

Because when your surroundings align with your goals, everything flows.

1. Why the Energy Around You Matters

Energy is contagious.

You don't just experience your environment—you **absorb it.** The spaces you occupy, the people you surround yourself with, and the content you consume are all shaping your thoughts, emotions, and mindset—**even when you don't realize it.**

- **Spend time with negative people?** You start absorbing their limiting beliefs.
- **Live in a chaotic, cluttered space?** Your mind feels just as scattered.
- **Constantly consume drama or toxic content?** You start seeing the world through that lens.

Your environment is always influencing you—it's up to you to make sure it's supporting your growth.

Signs Your Environment is Holding You Back:

You feel drained or uninspired after spending time with certain people.

Your space feels cluttered, messy, or stressful.

You keep falling into the same negative patterns.

You feel stuck, like something is holding you back but you can't figure out what.

If your environment is filled with **chaos, negativity, or distractions**, it's hard to **stay focused, motivated, and at peace.**

Signs Your Environment is Helping You Grow:

You feel at peace, clear-headed, and motivated.

The people around you challenge you in a good way.

Your space feels organized, calming, and aligned with your goals.

You are learning, expanding, and evolving.

When your environment **supports you**, it becomes a place that **inspires** you instead of draining you. You feel **clear, creative, and focused** because your surroundings match the life you're trying to build.

Your surroundings should reflect the life you want, not the life you're trying to escape from.

If your environment isn't aligned with where you want to go, **it's time to make some changes.**

Reflection Exercise:
- **Take an audit of your environment—your space, your relationships, your daily influences.**
- **What needs to change for it to better support your growth?**

You can't thrive in an environment that drains you. Create a space that fuels your success.

2. Marcello's Story – The Barbershop vs. The Salon (SNL Skit Explanation)

This example comes from a hilarious yet insightful skit from *Saturday Night Live (SNL)*, featuring a character named **Marcello** who experiences a stark contrast between two environments—a **barbershop** and a **salon**.

What Happens in the Skit?

Marcello, a young man, walks into a **barbershop** to get a haircut. From the moment he sits down, the **energy is intense.**

- The barbershop is filled with **loud conversations, roasting, and aggressive banter.**
- As soon as Marcello gets in the chair, the barber and other men start **teasing him about his height, his hairline, and random personal traits.**
- The jokes come fast, and even though they're meant to be *funny,* there's an edge to them that makes Marcello visibly uncomfortable.
- He tries to laugh along, but you can tell **he's not really enjoying it.**

The entire atmosphere is **hyper-masculine, competitive, and built on tearing each other down as a way of bonding.** It's not openly mean, but it's that type of humor where you have to be *tough enough* to handle it.

Marcello leaves the barbershop **feeling smaller, deflated, and subtly insecure.**

Later, Marcello finds himself at a **salon**—a completely different world.

- The moment he sits down, the energy is **warm, welcoming, and uplifting.**
- Instead of teasing him, the stylists **shower him with compliments** about his **skin, his hair, and his style.**
- The conversation is **supportive and positive.**
- The women in the salon **hype each other up, celebrate small wins, and genuinely make Marcello feel good about himself.**

As the compliments and positive energy surround him, Marcello's whole **demeanor changes.**

- He **sits up straighter.**
- His **confidence visibly grows.**
- He starts to **smile more and embrace the uplifting energy.**
- By the time he leaves the salon, he's **radiating confidence.**

Then, the **best part happens**—as he's about to leave, the stylists **tell him they miss him!**

- **"We missed you, Marcello!"** one of them says sweetly.
- Another stylist adds, **"Don't stay away too long next time."**
- The moment they say it, **Marcello literally blushes**—you can see how much it means to him.

It's such a small moment, but it speaks **volumes.**

- In the barbershop, he was just **another guy in the chair**—the vibe was all about who could handle the most roasting.
- In the salon, he was **seen, appreciated, and valued**—and it made all the difference.

Marcello **walks out of the salon feeling taller, happier, and more confident than ever.**

It's a funny but **shockingly real** contrast between how **different environments can either drain you or empower you.**

Marcello's Story – The Barbershop vs. The Salon: A Lesson in Self-Love and Environment

Marcello's experience is a **perfect example** of why self-love isn't just about what you do for yourself—it's also about **who and what you surround yourself with.**

This SNL skit highlights something many people never even stop to think about:

Your environment is shaping you, whether you realize it or not.

Marcello's experience in the **barbershop** made him feel **smaller.**

- The constant **teasing and jokes about his appearance** weren't just harmless fun—they slowly chipped away at his confidence.
- He tried to **laugh it off,** but deep down, he wasn't enjoying it.
- By the time he left, **he felt drained.**

The **salon,** on the other hand, made him feel **bigger.**

- Instead of tearing him down, the women **hyped him up.**
- Their compliments **built him up** rather than picking him apart.
- The moment they told him **they missed him,** he **blushed**—because for the first time, he truly felt **seen and valued.**
- He walked out **standing taller, feeling more confident, and glowing with self-assurance.**

And that's the lesson: The environments we choose either reinforce our insecurities or empower us.

How Energy Affects Self-Perception

The way people talk to us can either make us **shrink or stand taller.**

- The **barbershop's jokes** about Marcello's height weren't just jokes—they made him **second-guess himself.**
- Meanwhile, the **salon's compliments** made him feel **attractive, valued, and appreciated.**

Self-love isn't just about how you see yourself—it's about where you put yourself.

You can be the most confident person in the world, but if you're constantly in an environment that **diminishes you,** it will take a toll on you.

Practical Reflection: Ask yourself—

Are the people around you pointing out your flaws or highlighting your strengths?

Do they make you feel **taller or shorter?**

Do you **leave feeling good** about yourself, or do you leave **questioning your worth?**

The Importance of Choosing Uplifting Spaces

It's not about whether a place is **bad or good.** It's about whether it's **right for you.**

- Some men **thrive in the barbershop** energy.
- Others—like Marcello—feel **more at home in the salon.**

What matters is how YOU feel in the space.

Your Experience is Personal

- The **barbershop isn't bad, and the salon isn't better.**
- Some people **love the competitiveness of the barbershop.** Others feel **drained by it.**
- Some people **thrive in uplifting environments.** Others prefer **a tougher, grittier space.**
- **Neither is wrong**—the key is knowing **what works for YOU.**

Balancing Masculine & Feminine Energies

- Marcello felt **at home in the salon** because he was comfortable with **both masculine and feminine energy.**
- Other men may feel **more aligned with the barbershop.**
- **And that's okay.** The real power is in **self-awareness**—choosing what aligns with YOU.

Checking in with Yourself: Is Your Environment Helping or Hurting You?

Instead of forcing yourself to fit into a space just because it's *the norm,* ask:

Do I leave feeling drained or uplifted?

Do I feel like I have to shrink myself here, or do I feel like my full self?

Am I here because I want to be, or because I feel like I should be?

This ties beautifully into self-love as self-awareness.

You don't have to **follow the crowd.** You don't have to **stay somewhere that makes you feel small.**

You just have to follow what makes you feel good.

It's about paying attention to your energy and making choices that support it.

The Power of Being in the Right Environment

The best experiences happen when you're in a space that **matches your energy.**

- If you're forcing yourself into a space that doesn't align with you, you'll feel **out of place.**
- But when you're **where you belong,** everything flows **naturally.**

Why Energy Matters

- When a space is filled with people who **genuinely love being there,** the vibe is uplifting for everyone.
- Whether it's the **barbershop or the salon,** the right environment isn't just about the **place itself**—it's about the **collective energy of the people inside it.**

You Thrive Where You Feel Good

- Instead of trying to **force yourself to fit in,** focus on where you feel **energized and fulfilled.**
- When you're in a place that **supports your energy,** you become **part of the reason it feels so good to be there.**

Happiness in a space creates a better experience for everyone inside it.

That's self-love too—choosing places that allow you to show up as your full, happy self.

The Full-Circle Moment: Helping Others Find Their Own Alignment

When both the **barbershop and the salon** are filled with people who **genuinely enjoy being there,** everyone thrives.

It's not about one being better than the other—it's about alignment.

- Some people have **never even thought about their environment's impact** on them.
- But when they hear **stories like Marcello's,** they start to question it:
  Wait... maybe I feel drained all the time because I'm in the wrong space.

This is why perspective is everything.

- When we **share our experiences,** we help others **see new possibilities.**
- We give them **permission to try something different.**
- We encourage them to **step outside of what they've always known** and ask themselves:

Am I actually happy here?

Is this space making me feel like my best self?

What if I tried something different?

Marcello's example is powerful because it represents a moment of **realization.**

- He probably **never thought about the energy difference** until he actually **experienced it.**
- And when people hear that, they might start to **notice similar patterns in their own lives.**

3. Creating a Space (Physical & Mental) That Supports Your Growth

Your environment should be **a sanctuary, not a source of stress.** If your space **overwhelms you, drains you, or distracts you,** it's time to reset.

Your **physical** and **mental** space should work **for you, not against you.**

Physical Space:

Declutter your space.
- A messy room = a messy mind. When your surroundings are chaotic, your thoughts feel scattered too.
- Clear out what no longer serves you—**clothes, papers, old energy.**

Design your space for peace.
- Your space should feel **comforting, not chaotic.**
- **Soft lighting, candles, plants, scents, and colors** that make you feel **calm and inspired** can shift your mood instantly.

Surround yourself with inspiration.
- Create an **environment that reminds you of your goals.**
- Vision boards, books, quotes, or anything that **keeps you motivated and focused** belong in your space.

Mental Space:

Protect your mind.

- Be **intentional** about what you consume—**news, social media, music, conversations.**
- If something constantly leaves you feeling drained, uninspired, or anxious, **limit your exposure to it.**

Limit access to negative people.

- You don't owe **unlimited access** to anyone who drains your energy.
- Some people **only bring chaos, gossip, or doubt—**create boundaries that protect your peace.

Reframe your thoughts.

- Pay attention to **negative self-talk.** Would you say those things to your best friend?
- When you catch yourself spiraling, **shift the narrative.** Instead of "I can't do this," try "I'm figuring this out."

Your space should make you feel safe, empowered, and in control of your energy.

The goal isn't **perfection**—it's creating an environment that makes it easier to **thrive, not just survive.**

Reflection Exercise:

- **What's one small change you can make to your physical or mental space today to create more peace?**

Your environment should reflect the life you're building—not the one you're leaving behind.

4. Breaking Free from Negative Cycles & Toxic Influences

Sometimes, the biggest thing holding you back is what you refuse to let go of.

Toxic cycles aren't just about **relationships**—they show up in **habits, routines, and daily patterns** that quietly keep you stuck. Whether it's **self-sabotage, procrastination, negative thinking, or draining people**, these patterns shape your reality more than you realize.

Breaking free starts with awareness. The things you tolerate today will define your future.

How to Break Free:

Step 1: Identify the Cycle

- Are you always **saying yes when you want to say no?**
- Do you keep **surrounding yourself with the same draining energy?**
- Are you stuck in **procrastination, bad habits, or self-sabotage?**
- Do you always go back to **people, places, or routines that keep you in the same cycle?**

Step 2: Get Real About the Impact

- How is this cycle making you **feel?**
- Is it **helping you grow** or **keeping you small?**
- What would your life **look like without it?**

Step 3: Set Boundaries & Replace the Pattern

- **Create clear boundaries** for yourself and others.
- **Replace the toxic habit** with something that supports your growth.
- If it's a **person**—distance yourself. If it's a **habit**—replace it with a better one.
- **Make a new rule for yourself.** Example: *"I no longer engage in conversations that drain me."*

The moment you change your environment, you change your life.

You can't **grow in the same space that keeps you small**. Whether it's your **mindset, relationships, habits, or physical surroundings**, upgrading your life starts with **removing what no longer serves you**.

Reflection Exercise:

- **What's one toxic cycle you're ready to break?**
- **How will you take the first step today?**

Your environment shapes you—make sure it's shaping you into the person you want to become.

Final Thoughts: Your Environment = Your Growth

Your surroundings are shaping you—make sure they're shaping you into who you want to be.

Your space should be peaceful, your relationships should be supportive, and your habits should reflect your highest self.

If something feels off, change it. If something is draining you, release it. If something isn't serving you, walk away.

Your **environment** is either pushing you forward or holding you back—**there is no in-between.**

You are not meant to thrive in an environment that doesn't support your growth.

The moment you start creating a **space that aligns with your future,** everything else will follow.

Affirmation:

"I create a space—physically, mentally, and emotionally—that supports my peace, success, and growth."

This chapter is a whole energy shift. It's about making sure **everything around you is aligned with where you're going, not where you've been.**

This is about **choosing spaces that pour into you, protect your energy, and elevate your self-love.**

You don't have to stay where you've outgrown. Your best environment is the one that makes you feel like your best self.

Chapter 18: Customizing Life Lessons to Work for You

Life is **constantly** teaching you something. Every experience—**good or bad**—carries a lesson. But here's the key: **It's not just about what happens to you; it's about what you do with it.**

Some people **let life's challenges break them down.** Others use those same experiences to **level up.**

The difference? Mindset.

Your growth isn't about what you go through—it's about what you take from it.

Every setback, every success, every disappointment, and every win has something to offer. But not every lesson is **one-size-fits-all.** What works for someone else may not be the best path for you—and that's okay.

This chapter is about:

Shifting your perspective to see everything as an opportunity to grow.

Learning how to pick up the right skills for different areas of life.

Making sure every lesson you learn actually works for you.

Because when you learn to **adapt** and use knowledge to your advantage, you stop feeling like life is **happening to you**—and start making life **work for you.**

1. Viewing Everything as an Opportunity to Grow

Life will test you. That's a given.

Challenges, disappointments, and setbacks are part of the journey. **You can't avoid them—but you can control how you respond to them.**

Instead of asking, **"Why is this happening to me?"** start asking: *"What is this trying to teach me?"*

Every experience—good or bad—has **a lesson hidden inside it.** When you shift from **victim mode to growth mode**, you stop seeing struggles as **punishments** and start seeing them as **stepping stones.**

Reframing Life's Lessons:

Rejection → Redirection to something better.

- That job you didn't get, that person who walked away—it wasn't rejection, it was *protection.*
- The closed door wasn't a loss—it was life guiding you toward something that actually aligns with you.

Failure → Feedback for improvement.

- Every mistake holds a clue on how to do better next time.
- The only real failure is **not learning from the experience.**

Heartbreak → A lesson in self-worth and boundaries.

- Some people come into your life **to show you what you deserve—by being the example of what you don't.**
- When you learn from heartbreak, you stop settling for less and start choosing yourself first.

Obstacles → A chance to build resilience and problem-solving skills.

- Challenges force you to think differently, get creative, and grow stronger.

- When you overcome something difficult, you walk away **wiser, tougher, and more capable.**

Everything can teach you something—if you're willing to learn.
Nothing you go through is **wasted** if you take the lesson with you. **Every setback, every loss, every detour is shaping you into the person you're meant to be.**

Reflection Exercise:
- **Think of a past challenge that at first felt like a setback.**
- **What did you eventually learn from it?**
- **How did it shape you into who you are today?**

Growth isn't about avoiding struggles—it's about turning them into wisdom.

2. Learning the Right Skills & Perspectives for Different Areas of Life

Success in any area of life isn't about luck—it's about skills.
No one is born **knowing how to navigate life perfectly.** The difference between people who **thrive** and those who **struggle** isn't intelligence, talent, or luck—it's about **learning the right skills for the right situations.**

The key? Knowing what skills **matter most** in different areas of life. When you focus on **developing the right abilities**, you become **more adaptable, confident, and prepared** for anything life throws your way.

Essential Life Skills to Master:

For Mental & Emotional Strength:
    Emotional regulation – Learning to manage stress, anxiety, and emotions without letting them control you.
    Self-awareness – Understanding your triggers, patterns, and the areas where you need to grow.
    Perspective-shifting – Training your mind to **see problems differently** instead of reacting emotionally.

For Career & Success:
    Adaptability – Being flexible and open to **learning new things quickly.**
    Communication – Knowing how to **express yourself clearly**, whether in emails, meetings, or conversations.
    Strategic thinking – Making choices that **align with long-term goals** instead of just short-term comfort.

For Relationships & Social Growth:
    Boundaries – Understanding **what you will and won't tolerate** from others.
    Active listening – Actually **hearing and understanding** people, instead of just waiting for your turn to speak.
    Conflict resolution – Solving issues **without unnecessary drama**, reacting emotionally, or avoiding confrontation.

The more skills you learn, the more prepared you are for anything life throws at you.

Instead of **fearing challenges**, you'll know you have the **tools** to handle them. **Everything becomes easier when you're equipped with the right skill set.**

Reflection Exercise:
- **What's one life skill you feel could improve your life right now?**
- **How can you start developing it?**

Your future success isn't just about what happens to you—it's about what you've trained yourself to handle.

3. How to Adapt & Use Knowledge to Your Advantage
Knowledge is useless if you don't know how to apply it.

Some people are stuck in **"learning mode" forever**—reading books, watching videos, listening to advice, collecting information—but **never actually using it.** They know all the theories, but their life stays the same.

Then there are people who **adapt quickly, take action, and get results.**

The secret? Learning how to customize information so it actually works for YOU.

Not every lesson, strategy, or life hack applies **exactly as it is** to your situation. **Your job is to take what fits, adjust it, and make it your own.**

How to Make Knowledge Work for You:
Filter what applies to your life.
- Not every piece of advice is for you.

- Some things make sense for others but don't align with your situation. **Learn to take what fits and leave what doesn't.**

Experiment and adjust.

- Try new things, but make them work for you.
- If a strategy isn't working, **tweak it instead of giving up completely.**
- Example: If a morning routine doesn't fit your schedule, adjust it instead of ditching the idea of having one.

Take action.

- Stop waiting for the "perfect" plan—**use what you already know and start now.**
- You don't need **more information**, you need **more implementation.**

Real growth comes from applying knowledge, not just collecting it.

You don't need to **"know more"** to change your life. You need to **do more** with what you already know.

Reflection Exercise:

- **What's something you've learned recently that you haven't applied yet?**
- **What's one step you can take today to use it?**

Knowledge isn't power—applied knowledge is.

Final Thoughts: Make Life Work for You

Life is always teaching you something—you just have to pay attention.

Every experience, every mistake, every lesson is fuel for your growth.

The more you adapt and apply knowledge, the more life starts working in your favor.

So the question is: Are you going to sit back and watch life happen, or are you going to take control and make life work for you?

At the end of the day, **growth isn't about what happens to you—it's about what you do with it.** The lessons are there. The knowledge is available. **The power to change your life is already in your hands.**

The only thing left? **Taking action.**

Affirmation:

"I turn every experience into a lesson. I adapt, apply, and grow. Life works for me because I know how to make it work."

Part 4: Stepping Into Your Power

Self-love isn't just about feeling good—it's about **reclaiming your power** and **stepping into the life you deserve.** It's about realizing that you are not just a side character in your own story, passively waiting for life to happen to you. **You are the author.** And the moment you recognize that, everything changes.

This part of the book is where we take everything you've learned so far and **turn it into action.** This is where self-love stops being just an internal feeling and becomes a **way of moving through the world**—with confidence, intention, and unshakable self-trust.

What It Means to Step Into Your Power

Owning your power isn't about forcing confidence or performing strength—it's about **knowing yourself so deeply** that you no longer seek permission, validation, or approval from external sources. It's about standing firm in who you are, **without shrinking, apologizing, or dimming your light for anyone.**

True self-love means **owning your evolution.** It means realizing that your transformation starts from within—**your thoughts, your beliefs, and the way you see yourself.** Your glow-up begins in your mind before it ever shows up in your reality.

Stepping into your power looks like:

Breaking free from external validation. You stop basing your worth on what others think. You don't need anyone else's approval to feel whole.

Embracing your softness as a strength. Being kind, emotional, or nurturing is not weakness—it's power. You don't have to be hardened by life to be powerful.

Rewriting your narrative. The old stories you've told yourself—about who you are, what you deserve, and what's possible—are just that: old. You have full permission to rewrite them.

Moving with confidence, even before you "feel" ready. Confidence isn't about having zero doubts. It's about betting on yourself anyway.

This is the part where you stop **waiting.**

You are not waiting for permission.

You are not waiting for the "right time."

You are not waiting for someone else to tell you that you are worthy.

You already are. Right now. Exactly as you are.

The Power of Choice: Reclaiming Control Over Your Life

So much of stepping into your power is about **realizing that you always have a choice.**

You can choose to change the way you think about yourself.

You can choose to stop entertaining things that drain you.

You can choose to show up for yourself every single day.

Your life is not something happening *to* you—it's something you are **actively creating.** Every boundary you set, every decision you make, every thought you shift **is you reclaiming your power.**

And the more you make choices that align with your highest self, the stronger and more confident you become.

What You'll Learn in This Section

This section will guide you through the **mental, emotional, and energetic shifts** that will help you step into your power **unapologetically.**

How to let go of what doesn't serve you—people, habits, mindsets, and fears that keep you small.

How to romanticize your life—so every day feels full of beauty, magic, and intention.

How to balance your feminine and masculine energy—so you can flow with ease while still taking action toward your goals.

How to reinvent yourself at any time—because you are not stuck in any version of yourself that no longer aligns.

This is where you stop living by default and start **creating a life that feels aligned, exciting, and true to you.**

The Next Level Version of You is Already Within You

The version of you that is powerful, confident, and completely self-assured? **It already exists.** It's not some distant version of you that you'll "become" once you achieve, change, or prove yourself.

It's already inside of you.

You just have to start acting like her.

So the question is: Are you ready to step into it?

This is your moment. **Step into it.**

Chapter 19: The Art of Not Giving a F*ck – Freeing Yourself from External Validation

Let's be honest—**the biggest prison most people live in is the fear of what others will think.**

- You hesitate before posting something.
- You overthink your outfit because of what *"they"* might say.
- You hold back on pursuing your dreams because you're worried about judgment.

But here's the truth: *People's opinions of you say more about them than they do about you.*

Think about it:

- **Someone who is insecure** will judge confidence.
- **Someone who settles** will criticize ambition.
- **Someone who fears standing out** will shame those who shine.

So, ask yourself: **Are you really going to shrink yourself for people who don't even have their own life together?**

The Ultimate Flex?

Being so secure in yourself that outside opinions don't shake you.

Because when you finally stop living for validation, you:

Stop over-explaining yourself.

Make bold decisions without fear.

Move with confidence, even when people don't "get" you.
Free yourself from the need to be liked.
And that? That's true self-love.

1. Why Do We Care So Much About Other People's Opinions?

Spoiler alert: Most of us have been trained since childhood to seek validation.

From an early age, we were taught that **approval equals acceptance.** Whether it was at home, in school, or in social circles, we were conditioned to believe that **our worth was tied to how well we fit in.**

- You were praised for being the **"good kid"** who followed the rules.
- You were told to **"be polite,"** even when it meant suppressing your true feelings.
- You learned that making others comfortable was **more important than expressing your real self.**

And at the time? **It made sense.**

Back then, validation meant safety. If you were liked, approved of, and accepted, you belonged. You were protected. It was an instinct for survival—because being rejected or standing out too much could mean being excluded, and as social creatures, **belonging feels like a necessity.**

But as an adult? **Constantly looking for approval is a trap.**

The Biggest Fear Behind External Validation? Rejection.

Most people don't seek validation because they **need** approval. They seek it because they **fear rejection.**

- They fear losing relationships.
- They fear judgment.
- They fear failure.
- They fear standing alone.

And so, they **play small.** They hold back. They filter themselves to fit in. **They silence parts of who they are just to be accepted.**

But Here's the Real Question:

Would you rather...

Be **accepted** for a version of yourself that isn't real?

Or be **truly happy and authentic**—even if it means not everyone approves?

Because at the end of the day, **real freedom isn't about getting everyone to like you.**

It's about realizing **you don't need validation to be worthy.**

The Harsh Truth:

- No matter what you do, **someone will have an opinion.**
- No matter how hard you try, **you can't please everyone.**
- And even if you **live your whole life for others,** some people **will still find a reason to judge.**

So why waste energy **chasing approval that doesn't matter?**

Why live your life for people who **aren't even living fully themselves?**

When You Stop Caring About External Approval, You Start Living for YOU.

When you **free yourself from the need to be liked,** you unlock a level of confidence that **most people will never experience.**

- You stop filtering your personality just to be accepted.
- You start making choices based on what **you actually want,** not what's expected.
- You walk through life with **authenticity and peace,** instead of anxiety and overthinking.

The **ultimate flex?** *Knowing you're already enough—without needing anyone else to confirm it.*

2. The Price of Seeking Validation – And Why It's Not Worth It

Living for external validation will cost you more than you realize.

The need for approval doesn't just shape your choices—it **steals your peace, your authenticity, and your dreams.** You start living for **others' expectations instead of your own desires.**

Here's what you're really sacrificing when you let external opinions control you:

Your Peace – You'll constantly feel **anxious about what others think,** overanalyzing every decision instead of just *living.*

- Every post, every outfit, every opinion becomes a mental battle of *"Will they approve?"*

- You'll never feel fully secure because your confidence depends on *other people's reactions,* which are **out of your control.**

Your Authenticity – You'll shape-shift into whatever version of yourself gets the most approval, losing who you *actually* are.

- You'll **edit yourself down** just to fit into other people's comfort zones.
- You'll stop doing things that genuinely **light you up** just because they might not be "cool" or widely accepted.
- You'll slowly lose your unique spark, **turning into a watered-down version of yourself** just to keep others happy.

Your Dreams – You'll hesitate to go after what you *truly* want because someone might judge you for it.

- You won't start the business because *what if it fails?*
- You won't post that content because *what if people don't like it?*
- You won't make that bold move because *what will they say?*
- And before you know it, **your entire life is based on avoiding judgment instead of chasing fulfillment.**

And the irony? Even if you do everything "right," people will still talk.

You could spend your entire life **trying to be "perfect,"** and people would STILL find something to say.

- If you **play it safe,** they'll say you're boring.

- If you **take risks,** they'll say you're reckless.
- If you **stay quiet,** they'll assume things about you.
- If you **speak up,** they'll say you talk too much.

You can't win a game that was never meant for you to win.
So why even play?

Why waste time obsessing over **how others see you,** when you could be spending that energy **building a life that makes YOU happy?**

So why not just do whatever makes YOU happy?

At the end of the day, **judgment is unavoidable.** You might as well **live for yourself.**

The people who **truly support you** will stick around. **The ones who don't?** They were never meant to be part of your journey anyway.

Your life, your rules. The only validation you need is your own.

The moment you stop needing outside approval, **you unlock a level of freedom, confidence, and peace that most people will never experience.**

3. How to Stop Giving a F*ck & Start Living For YOU

Confidence isn't about having no doubts—it's about trusting yourself despite them.

Fear of judgment is normal. But **letting it control your life?** That's a choice. And the best choice you can make? **Living for YOU, not for the approval of others.**

Here's how to break free from the **validation trap** and start **moving like the main character** in your own life.

Identify Where You're Still Seeking Validation
Self-awareness is the first step to freedom.
Ask yourself:

- Do you **need likes, comments, or approval** to feel good about yourself?
- Do you **hold back your opinions** because you're afraid of disagreement?
- Do you **fear standing out** because you don't want to be judged?

Once you spot where you're giving away your power, you can take it back.

The areas where you **hesitate the most** are usually the areas where you need to trust yourself more. The more you notice where you're holding back, the easier it becomes to **break free from the need for outside approval.**

Detach from Needing Approval
Not everyone will like you—and that's a good thing.
Imagine how **exhausting** it would be to **please everyone.** You'd be constantly shifting, changing, and bending yourself just to fit into other people's expectations.
But here's the truth:
Your worth isn't up for debate. You are already enough, whether people recognize it or not.

Don't internalize other people's insecurities. If someone projects negativity onto you, that's *their* issue—not yours.

Rejection isn't a reflection of your value. Sometimes people don't understand your path, and that's okay. **You don't need their approval to keep moving forward.**

Once you stop needing external validation, you become untouchable.

The moment you realize **you don't need to be liked to be successful, happy, or fulfilled**, you start showing up as your **true self—boldly and unapologetically.**

Own Your Decisions With Confidence

If you want to stop caring about what others think, start standing in your truth—unapologetically.

- **Stop over-explaining yourself.** You don't owe people an essay on why you're making a choice.
- **Make bold moves without waiting for permission.** If it feels right to YOU, that's enough.
- **Stand in your truth even when it makes others uncomfortable.** Their discomfort is not your responsibility.
- **Be okay with being misunderstood.** You don't have to correct every false assumption about you.

Move like the main character, because that's exactly who you are.

Confidence isn't about **never doubting yourself.** It's about **making decisions that align with YOU, even when others don't get it.**

Filter Opinions—Only Take Advice from People You Admire

Rule of thumb: Don't take criticism from people who haven't done what you're trying to do.

People love to give opinions—but **not all opinions are valid.**

Before you take advice from someone, ask yourself:

Is this person where I want to be? If not, why does their opinion hold weight?

Have they built something for themselves? If they've never taken risks, why are they critiquing your path?

Are they happy, secure, and fulfilled? If they're miserable, broke, or insecure, why are they giving you life advice?

If you wouldn't switch places with them, don't take their advice.

So many people hold back because they're **worried about the opinions of people who don't even have their own life together.**

The only opinions that matter are the ones that align with your growth, vision, and happiness.

Thought: When you stop living for external validation, you unlock a level of confidence, freedom, and peace that most people will never experience. **You owe it to yourself to stop giving a f*ck and start living.**

4. Reprogramming Your Mind: Shifting From Validation-Seeker to Unshakable

Your brain is wired to seek validation—but you can rewire it.

Since childhood, you've been conditioned to look **outside yourself** for approval. Society, family, school, and social media have trained you to believe that your worth is measured by how much others approve of you. **But here's the truth:**

External validation is a trap—it's never enough.

You'll always feel the need for more approval, more likes, more reassurance. **Until you realize that the only validation that actually matters is your own.**

So how do you break the cycle? **You start training yourself to trust your own judgment over outside opinions.**

Steps to Shift from Validation-Seeker to Unshakable:

Start Small: Make one decision without checking in with anyone first.

- Stop waiting for permission. **Trust yourself.** If you want to wear something bold, post a certain picture, or make a life change—**do it without asking for approval.**

- The more you prove to yourself that you can make good decisions without outside input, the more confidence you build.

Change Your Self-Talk: Instead of "What will they think?" ask "What do I want?"

- Pay attention to the way you talk to yourself. **Are your thoughts centered around what others will think?** If so, shift them.

- Instead of worrying about others' opinions, **ask yourself what aligns with YOUR happiness, goals, and values.**

Practice Silence: Let people assume whatever they want. No explanation needed.

- **Not everything needs to be explained, defended, or justified.**
- Sometimes, the best response is **no response.** Let people talk, let them speculate—**your life doesn't require their approval.**
- The moment you stop over-explaining, you take your power back.

Surround Yourself with Confident Energy: Be around people who own who they are—that energy is contagious.

- **Confidence is learned.** When you surround yourself with people who walk through life unapologetically, **you absorb that energy.**
- Observe how they move, how they speak, and how they make decisions **without fear of judgment.**
- When you're around people who prioritize **self-trust over external approval,** you naturally start doing the same.

Detach from the Outcome: Not Everyone Will Like You— and That's a Good Thing.

- The biggest breakthrough? **Realizing that not everyone's opinion matters.**
- The people who judge you or don't support you? **They were never meant to be part of your journey.**

- Trying to please everyone **dilutes your authenticity.** The right people will be drawn to the real you.

Self-validation is a muscle. The more you practice, the stronger it gets.

You don't wake up one day and suddenly stop caring about opinions—it's a process. **But every time you choose yourself over external approval, you take a step closer to true confidence.**

Because once you stop **waiting for permission** to be yourself, you become **unstoppable.**

Final Thoughts: The Ultimate Glow-Up is Not Giving a F*ck

There is NOTHING more attractive, magnetic, or powerful than someone who is completely at peace with themselves.

The moment you stop living for validation, you start living for REAL.

You are already enough. No outside approval required.

So go be loud. Be bold. Be messy. Be fully YOU.

The world will adjust.

Affirmation:

"I do not seek approval. I trust myself fully. I live for ME, not for validation."

Chapter 20: Softness is Strength – Embracing Your Feminine & Masculine Energy

For too long, we've been conditioned to believe that **strength means hardness.** That to survive in this world, we need to be **tough, guarded, and emotionally detached.** That being "soft" makes you weak. That vulnerability is a liability. That only those who push, force, and dominate will succeed.

But here's the truth: *True strength is about balance.*

It's not about being **overly rigid or endlessly passive.** It's about knowing when to **stand firm** and when to **surrender.** When to **lead with logic** and when to **trust your intuition.** When to **fight for something** and when to **let go and flow.**

Strength is fluid. It's the ability to adapt.

Knowing when to be firm and when to be fluid.

Knowing when to push and when to let things flow.

Knowing when to protect yourself and when to receive love.

Real power is being able to shift between your masculine and feminine energy—using both as tools to navigate life.

Because if you only operate from **one,** you're **limiting yourself.**

Some people are stuck in **hyper-masculine energy**—always **pushing, forcing, controlling, and overworking,** afraid to soften. Others are stuck in **wounded feminine energy—afraid to take action, overly passive, or constantly seeking external validation.**

But the most **magnetic, successful, and empowered people?** They know how to **balance both.** They can be **soft without being weak.** They can be **strong without being cold.**

This chapter is about:

Breaking free from survival mode.

Understanding when to tap into your feminine and masculine energy.

Using this balance to live your most magnetic, empowered life.

Because **mastering both energies** isn't just the key to confidence and success—it's the key to a **life that flows effortlessly in your favor.**

1. Understanding Feminine & Masculine Energy – You Have Both

Let's get something straight: **Feminine and masculine energy have nothing to do with gender.**

Everyone—no matter their gender—has both energies inside them.

These energies are not about being "male" or "female." They are **different modes of operating, different strengths to tap into.** The key is learning how to use them **intentionally** and in **harmony.**

When you master both, **you become adaptable, balanced, and magnetic.** You can **hustle when needed, but also flow when it's time to receive.** You can **set boundaries with strength, but also move with grace.**

Feminine Energy (Flow, Intuition, Receiving, Creation)
Strengths:
  - Softness, intuition, patience, creativity, surrender, trust, emotional intelligence.

- It's **nurturing, flowing, and deeply connected to emotions and intuition.**

High-vibe feminine energy looks like:
- **Trusting the process** instead of trying to control everything.
- **Being open to receiving** love, help, and abundance.
- **Moving with ease** instead of forcing things.
- **Honoring your emotions** instead of suppressing them.
- **Enjoying the present moment** instead of always being in grind mode.

Wounded feminine energy looks like:
- **People-pleasing and lack of boundaries**—sacrificing yourself for others.
- **Struggling to take action**—waiting for things to happen instead of making moves.
- **Staying stuck in victim mentality**—feeling powerless and dependent.

Masculine Energy (Action, Protection, Structure, Leadership)

Strengths:
- Discipline, logic, focus, decisiveness, goal-setting, structure, stability.
- It's **driven, protective, and provides direction and foundation.**

High-vibe masculine energy looks like:

- **Setting and enforcing boundaries** without guilt.
- **Making bold decisions and taking action,** even when you're scared.
- **Providing structure for yourself** (routines, planning, accountability).
- **Protecting your energy**—knowing when to say *NO*.
- **Leading with confidence** instead of waiting for direction.

Wounded masculine energy looks like:

- **Being overly controlling**—needing to force everything.
- **Operating in hustle mode 24/7** with no rest.
- **Suppressing emotions**—thinking feelings = weakness.
- **Using aggression** instead of healthy assertion.

Neither energy is "better" than the other. They are tools. And when used together? **They make you unstoppable.**

Masculine energy helps you take action.

Feminine energy helps you trust the flow.

Masculine energy builds the foundation.

Feminine energy brings creativity and life to it.

When you know how to **balance both energies**, you become a force—**powerful, peaceful, and in control of your life.**

2. How Society Conditions Us to Be Out of Balance

Most people are operating in an energy imbalance—either too much masculine or too much feminine.

Why? **Because society has trained us to reject balance.**

Instead of embracing **both energies**, we're pushed into one extreme or the other—often in ways that keep us stuck in **struggle, burnout, or emotional disconnection.**

In Work & Success? Society Pushes Us Into Toxic Hustle Culture.

We're taught that **success = grind mode 24/7.** That **resting is weakness** and **overworking is a badge of honor.**

Masculine Energy Overload:

- Always grinding, always in "go mode," never slowing down.
- Prioritizing **logic and results over intuition and creativity.**
- Suppressing emotions in favor of **"getting things done."**
- Feeling guilty for slowing down, as if rest = failure.

The result? Burnout, disconnection from self, and an inability to enjoy success once we achieve it.

In Relationships? People Often Lean Too Much Into One Energy.

In relationships, **imbalanced energy** leads to unhealthy dynamics:

Overly masculine?

- Struggles with **vulnerability**—always feeling the need to be "strong."
- Struggles with **receiving love**—believes they must always be the giver, protector, or provider.
- Feels the need to **control or lead everything**, which blocks intimacy and emotional connection.

Overly feminine?
- **Lacks boundaries**—lets people walk all over them in the name of "love" or "keeping the peace."
- Waits for someone to **"save" them** instead of taking action.
- Avoids making decisions, instead **deferring to others for direction.**

The result? Power struggles, unfulfilled relationships, and feeling drained from either **giving too much** or **not taking enough control of your life.**

But Real Power is in Balance.

True strength isn't about **only being masculine** or **only being feminine.** It's about knowing **when to lead and take action (masculine) and when to surrender and trust (feminine).**

The goal isn't to be one or the other—it's to be BOTH, effortlessly.

- **Masculine energy helps you create structure and take action.**
- **Feminine energy helps you trust, flow, and receive with ease.**

When you learn to shift between both energies, life starts flowing instead of feeling like a constant fight.

3. How to Balance Your Feminine & Masculine Energy for Maximum Power

Step 1: Identify Your Dominant Energy

Ask yourself:

- **Do you find it easier to take action but struggle with letting go and trusting?** → You might be **too in your masculine.**
- **Do you find it easier to flow and receive but struggle with making moves and setting boundaries?** → You might be **too in your feminine.**

Awareness is key. Once you recognize your imbalance, you can start integrating the energy you need more of.

Step 2: Integrate the Opposite Energy

If you're too in your masculine (always in control, always in hustle mode):

- **Start practicing trust**—not everything needs to be micromanaged.
- **Spend more time in creativity, stillness, and intuition**—let yourself explore, daydream, and listen to your inner voice.
- **Allow yourself to receive**—love, compliments, and help—without guilt. You don't have to do everything alone.

If you're too in your feminine (struggle with taking action, lack structure & boundaries):

- **Set clear boundaries and say NO more often**—protect your energy.
- **Take action—even if you don't feel "ready"**—waiting for the perfect moment is just fear in disguise.
- **Build self-discipline**—create morning routines, set goals, and stick to commitments even when you don't feel like it.

Step 3: Daily Practices to Balance Your Energy

To Tap into Your Feminine Energy (Flow, Trust, Intuition):

- Move slower—stop rushing everything. **Slow down and be present.**
- Practice surrender—**trust that good things are flowing to you** without forcing them.
- Do things that feel soft & nourishing—**bubble baths, journaling, dancing, walking in nature, reading, meditating.**

To Tap into Your Masculine Energy (Discipline, Action, Structure):

- Set daily goals—and actually execute them. **Masculine energy is about taking action, not just planning.**
- Stop waiting for "the right time" and **just DO IT.** Perfectionism = procrastination.
- Assert yourself—**set boundaries with confidence and speak up for what you need.**

A fully balanced person knows how to shift between these energies effortlessly.

They **know when to lead and when to trust.**

They **know when to take action and when to flow.**

They **know how to be powerful without being forceful and soft without being weak.**

This is the true key to personal magnetism, success, and deep self-mastery.

4. The Magnetic Power of Balancing These Energies

When you master the balance between your **masculine and feminine energy**, you **stop forcing** and start **flowing.** You **become magnetic**—naturally attracting success, love, and fulfillment without burnout or struggle.

In Work & Success:

You **take action** and make bold moves (**masculine**) but **trust the process** instead of obsessively controlling every detail (**feminine**).

You **work hard** and stay disciplined (**masculine**) but also **allow yourself to rest, celebrate wins, and receive rewards** without guilt (**feminine**).

You **stay focused on goals** (**masculine**) while also **tapping into creativity and intuition** to guide your path (**feminine**).

The result? You become an unstoppable force—**productive but not burnt out, ambitious but still at peace.**

In Relationships:

You know when to **assert yourself and set boundaries** (**masculine**) but also when to **be soft, open, and receptive** (**feminine**).

You don't **overgive or overextend**—you understand the **power of reciprocity** in love.

You don't feel the need to **control everything**—you trust, surrender, and allow things to flow naturally.

You attract healthy, balanced relationships because **you are in balance yourself.**

The result? You experience **deeper intimacy, mutual respect, and relationships that feel easy—not forced.**

In Life Overall:

You feel **powerful but peaceful—strong without being rigid, soft without being weak.**

You no longer operate from **fear, control, or burnout.** Instead, you move with **confidence and trust.**

You attract **people and experiences that match your balanced energy.**

You radiate **calm certainty, self-assuredness, and ease.**

The result? Life feels like it's **flowing in your favor,** not something you have to fight against.

When you master both energies, you become magnetic.

You walk into a room, and people **feel** your presence before you even say a word.

You stop chasing—opportunities, people, and success start coming to you.

You move through life with **confidence, grace, and ease.**

This is what it means to embody true power.

Final Thoughts: The Strength of Softness

Softness isn't weakness—it's power.

Action without trust is force. Trust without action is wishful thinking. You need BOTH.

When you learn to balance these energies, you unlock a whole new level of confidence, success, and peace.

So, are you ready to step into your full power?

The moment you stop operating from **one extreme** and embrace the **full spectrum of your strength,** you'll notice everything around you shift.

- You'll **attract** what aligns instead of chasing what doesn't.
- You'll **trust yourself** enough to take action—but also trust life enough to let things unfold.
- You'll **feel more at peace, more magnetic, and more unstoppable** than ever before.

True power is knowing when to move and when to let things move toward you. Master both, and life starts working in your favor.

Affirmation:

"I embrace both my strength and my softness. I know when to take action and when to trust. I am fully balanced, fully powerful, and fully at peace."

Chapter 21: The Glow-Up is Mental First – The Power of Reinventing Yourself

A real glow-up isn't just **losing weight, getting a new hairstyle,** or upgrading your wardrobe.

It's not just about aesthetics. **You can change everything on the outside and still feel lost inside.**

The real glow-up is mental.

Before your life changes, your mindset has to change.

Because here's the truth:

- You can buy **new clothes**, get in **the best shape of your life**, and **still feel insecure.**

- You can achieve **success**, make **more money**, and **still doubt yourself.**

- You can be in a **relationship**, have someone love you, and **still feel unworthy.**

The ultimate glow-up is about becoming unshakable from the inside out.

It's about self-worth that isn't based on external validation.

It's about confidence that isn't dependent on how others see you.

It's about emotional strength that allows you to handle anything life throws at you.

This chapter is about **reinventing yourself from the core—** mentally, emotionally, and energetically.

Because once you change **how you think, how you see yourself, and how you carry yourself...** everything else follows.

Your mindset is the foundation of your glow-up. Build it strong, and nothing can shake you.

1. Why the Glow-Up Starts in Your Mind First

If your mind doesn't evolve, your reality won't either.

No matter how much you change externally, **if your mindset remains the same, your life will stay the same.**

- You can upgrade your looks, but if you **still see yourself as unworthy,** you won't feel any different.
- You can land your dream job, but if you **still struggle with imposter syndrome,** success won't feel satisfying.
- You can enter a new relationship, but if you **haven't healed past wounds,** you'll keep repeating old patterns.

A glow-up isn't just about looking different—it's about thinking differently.

You can't create a new reality with an old mindset.

- If your thoughts are full of self-doubt, you'll keep playing small.
- If your beliefs are rooted in fear, you'll keep hesitating instead of taking action.
- If your inner dialogue is negative, no amount of external validation will ever feel like enough.

The Real Glow-Up Happens When You Shift Internally

Think about this:

You **don't need to wait** until you *look the part* to **act like the part.**

You **don't need to wait** until you *feel confident* to **start moving with confidence.**

You **don't need validation** from anyone to decide that **you are worthy, right now.**

The people who **glow effortlessly** are the ones who **embody their highest self before the proof is there.**

- They walk with confidence before the success arrives.
- They believe in their worth before the world recognizes it.
- They make moves before they "feel ready."

Your glow-up begins the moment you start acting like the version of yourself you're becoming—before the results even show.

This isn't "fake it till you make it." This is **embodying your future self now**—training your mind and energy to match the life you want.

Transformation starts in the mind. Once you believe in yourself, the rest of the world has no choice but to follow.

2. The Formula for a True Mental Glow-Up

The secret? **You have to think, act, and move like the version of yourself you're trying to become.**

Your reality shifts the moment **you stop waiting** to feel ready and **start embodying your highest self now.**

Ask yourself: *If I was already THAT person, how would I show up today?*

Step 1: Rewrite Your Mental Programming

Your thoughts create your reality. If you want to level up, you need to **upgrade your mindset.**

Limiting beliefs to let go of:

"I'm not good enough." → "I am more than enough."

"I'll start when I'm ready." → "I start now. Growth happens in action."

"Success isn't for people like me." → "I create my own success."

Your mind will believe whatever you tell it—so feed it thoughts that support your glow-up.

Exercise: Write down the old beliefs that are keeping you stuck. Now, reframe them into powerful affirmations.

Step 2: Embody Confidence Before the Results Show Up

Confidence is not about how you look—it's about how you carry yourself.

You don't need to wait until you **feel confident** to **act confident.** Confidence isn't something you're born with—it's **a skill you build through action.**

How to Embody Confidence Daily:

Walk with purpose—head high, shoulders back. Your posture shifts your energy.

Speak with certainty—even if you're still learning. Own your voice.

Make eye contact—don't shrink yourself. Presence is power.

Stop over-explaining yourself—your choices don't need approval.

Take up space—you are not "too much." You are just enough.

The way you carry yourself tells the world how to treat you—act like you already belong.

Exercise: What's one way you can start showing up with confidence today, even if you don't feel "ready"?

Step 3: Detach from Your Past Identity

You don't owe anyone your "old self."

A lot of people **stay stuck** because they feel like they can't change.

They think:

- "What will people think if I start acting differently?"
- "They know me as this person—I can't suddenly level up."
- "I don't want to seem fake."

Here's the truth: You are allowed to evolve.

You **don't have to keep playing small** to make others comfortable.

You **don't have to stay stuck** just because people are used to you being that way.

You **don't need permission** to become the best version of yourself.

Decide who you want to be—and step into it unapologetically.

Exercise: What old identity, habit, or belief are you ready to release?

Step 4: Move Like Your Future Self

If you already were the best version of yourself, how would you act? What habits would you have? How would you think?

How to Start Moving Like Your Future Self Today:

- **Mindset:** Speak, think, and act like the person you're becoming.
- **Energy:** Surround yourself with people who reflect where you're going, not where you've been.
- **Habits:** Do things your highest self would do—wake up earlier, dress better, invest in yourself.
- **Boundaries:** Stop entertaining things that don't align with your vision.

Your future self is waiting for you to show up. Start now.

Exercise: Write down a "day in the life" of your highest self. How can you start embodying that version of you today?

The mental glow-up is the foundation for every other glow-up. Once your mind evolves, your reality has no choice but to follow.

3. The External Glow-Up Will Naturally Follow

Once you change your mindset, your external world WILL shift.

Your **thoughts, beliefs, and energy shape your reality.** When you **start thinking differently, you start acting differently.** And when you **start acting differently, your life begins to shift.**

Your Mindset Shapes Your Actions → Your Actions Shape Your Reality

Once you mentally step into **your highest self,** you will start naturally **aligning with that version of you.**

What happens when you embody the glow-up mentally first?

You'll start dressing like the person you want to be.

- You won't wait for a "special occasion" to show up as your best self.
- You'll naturally gravitate toward **clothing, hairstyles, and a presence that reflect your confidence.**
- You'll wear things that make YOU feel good instead of dressing to impress others.

You'll start making bolder moves.

- You'll **speak up for yourself** instead of holding back.
- You'll **go after what you want** instead of waiting for the "right" moment.
- You'll **apply for that job, start that project, leave that situation**—because you finally believe you are worthy of more.

You'll start attracting better opportunities and relationships.

- **People will feel your energy shift.** When you believe in yourself, others start believing in you too.
- **Toxic people will naturally fade away** because you won't tolerate what no longer aligns.

- **New doors will open**—opportunities, friendships, relationships that match your elevated mindset will come to you.

The way you treat yourself sets the tone for everything else.

If you see yourself as **worthy, valuable, and powerful**, you will:

- Take better care of yourself.
- Speak to yourself with love and respect.
- Set boundaries that protect your peace.
- Move through life with **grace, confidence, and certainty.**

If you **still see yourself as unworthy, doubtful, or "not enough,"** your external world will reflect that too—**low self-esteem, settling for less, tolerating what doesn't serve you.**

When your inner world is glowing, your outer world has no choice but to reflect it.

The true glow-up starts within. And once that transformation happens, the **physical glow-up becomes effortless.**

Final Thoughts: The Glow-Up is a Lifestyle

The ultimate glow-up isn't a look—it's a mindset.

- It's **not just about changing your appearance**—it's about changing how you see yourself.
- It's **not about waiting until you feel ready**—it's about stepping into your power now.
- It's **not about external validation**—it's about knowing your worth from the inside out.

When you shift internally, the world shifts with you.

- Your energy changes, and people feel it.

- Your actions change, and opportunities open up.
- Your standards change, and you start attracting better.

Confidence, success, and happiness come when you decide to embody them NOW.

- Not when you lose the weight.
- Not when you land the dream job.
- Not when someone else validates you.

So stop waiting for the glow-up—step into it. It's already yours.

Everything you want? **It's already within you.** The only thing left to do is **own it, embody it, and live it.**

Affirmation:

"I am glowing from the inside out. My energy is magnetic. I am stepping into my highest self daily."

Chapter 22: Romanticizing Your Life – Making Every Day Feel Like Main Character Energy

Let's get something straight: **Your life is already a movie.**

The problem? **You're not acting like the main character.**

You're waiting. **Waiting for the big moment—the perfect job, the dream relationship, the glow-up—to finally feel happy.**

But what if I told you **happiness isn't something you find—it's something you create?**

Romanticizing your life isn't about being delusional—it's about making every moment feel special, intentional, and exciting.

It's about **seeing the beauty in the ordinary.**

It's about **choosing joy, even in small moments.**

It's about **living with main character energy—on purpose.**

Because the truth is: **You are the main character. You always have been.**

It's time to start acting like it.

1. What Does It Mean to "Romanticize Your Life"?

It's not about ignoring reality—it's about shifting how you experience it.

Most people think happiness is **something you get later**—after you hit a big milestone, after life finally "gets good." But here's the truth:

You could have everything you ever wanted, but if you don't learn to enjoy life NOW, you never will.

Romanticizing your life means:

Finding magic in small, everyday moments. (Drinking your coffee like you're in a Parisian café, playing music while getting ready like it's a movie montage.)

Seeing yourself as the star of your own story. (Moving with confidence, making bold choices, embracing your uniqueness.)

Creating rituals that make life feel special. (Lighting candles while you journal, taking solo dates, dressing up just for you.)

Being fully present in the moment instead of waiting for "someday" to be happy.

Because the truth is:

- The dream job? Won't make you happy if you don't already appreciate your mornings.
- The relationship? Won't fulfill you if you don't know how to enjoy your own company.
- The glow-up? Won't feel satisfying if you don't already feel good in your own skin.

It's not about "having a perfect life"—it's about appreciating the one you have, while making it better.

Exercise: Think of one simple, ordinary moment in your day. How can you make it feel more special?

- Can you wake up a little earlier to enjoy the sunrise with your favorite music?
- Can you plate your food beautifully instead of just eating in a rush?
- Can you take a slow walk and appreciate the details around you?

Small shifts = a romanticized life. It starts now.

2. The Shift: Stop Waiting for Big Moments & Make Every Day a Vibe

Too many people **postpone happiness.** They tell themselves:

"I'll feel confident when I lose weight."

"I'll feel successful when I make more money."

"I'll be happy when I meet the right person."

But here's the truth: If you don't learn to enjoy the process, you won't enjoy the destination either.

No external achievement **will magically make you feel whole** if you haven't learned to **enjoy life now.**

The secret? **Stop waiting—start living.**

How to Start Romanticizing Your Life Now:

Treat daily routines like rituals.

- Don't just go through the motions—make them **intentional.**
- **Light a candle** while you journal.
- **Play your favorite music** while getting ready.
- **Sip your coffee or tea slowly** like you're in a European café.

Dress like the person you want to be.

- Even if you're just running errands, **step out like the main character.**
- Wear the perfume, put on the outfit—**because you deserve to feel good now.**

Capture small moments like they're cinematic.

- Take photos of **sunsets, city lights, cozy corners of your home.**
- Slow down and appreciate **how beautiful the little things really are.**

Speak to yourself like you're the protagonist.

- No more negative self-talk—you **are the lead role in this film.**
- Hype yourself up the way you would **your favorite character in a movie.**

Move with intention.

- Walk with **purpose** like you're stepping into a big scene.
- **Make eye contact.** Let your energy be felt.
- Stop rushing through life—**start living in it.**

When you stop waiting for happiness and start living with presence, everything changes.

The glow, the confidence, the joy? It was never about "someday." It's about now.

Exercise: What's one thing you do every day that you can start doing more intentionally?

- Can you make your morning routine feel more luxurious?
- Can you slow down and actually enjoy your meals instead of rushing?
- Can you take a moment to feel the sun on your face, appreciate fresh air, or just breathe deeply?

Main character energy isn't about a perfect life—it's about how you experience it.

3. Creating Main Character Energy – How to Move Like You're THAT Person

Main Character Energy isn't about being self-absorbed—it's about owning your presence.

It's about **stepping fully into your power** and carrying yourself like someone who **knows they belong, knows they are valuable, and knows they deserve good things.**

When you start moving with **that energy,** the world responds accordingly.

How to Move Like a Main Character:
Walk into every room with confidence.
- Not arrogance—just the quiet self-assurance of someone who **knows they belong.**
- Shoulders back, head high—**own your space.**

Make your life visually appealing.
- Keep your **home, workspace, and environment beautiful**—set the scene for your own movie.
- **Light candles, buy flowers, decorate your space, dress in ways that make you feel unstoppable.**

Create your own soundtrack.
- Build playlists that match the energy you want to feel— **soft and dreamy, bold and powerful, mysterious and intriguing.**

- Play music while you cook, drive, or get ready—**make it feel cinematic.**

Stop waiting for permission.

- Main characters don't ask if they're **"good enough"**— they **just are.**
- Take up space. Go for what you want. Speak your truth without hesitation.

Romanticize even the "boring" moments.

- Make **even simple things feel special**—reading in the sun, taking a slow morning, journaling with your favorite drink.
- Live like **every little moment is a scene in a movie**— because it is.

When you see yourself as the main character, your entire reality starts shifting to match that energy.

People start noticing you differently.

Opportunities start opening up.

You start attracting experiences that align with the energy you embody.

Because when you truly believe you're THAT person, the universe does too.

Exercise: If your life was a movie, what kind of main character would you be? **How can you embody that version of yourself now?**

- Would you be the **mysterious, confident one who walks with purpose?**

- The **soft, dreamy, romantic soul who finds beauty in everything?**
- The **bold, fearless one who takes risks and always follows their heart?**

Pick your energy, step into it, and let the world adjust.

4. Falling in Love with Your Own Company

If you don't love spending time with yourself, why would anyone else?

Most people fear solitude because they **mistake it for loneliness.** But being alone **isn't lonely when you enjoy your own energy.**

Learning to love your own company is the foundation of self-love.

The more you **nurture your relationship with yourself,** the less you'll depend on external validation to feel good. You'll become so fulfilled **on your own** that anyone who enters your life is simply a **bonus, not a necessity.**

How to Make Solo Time Feel Luxurious:

Take yourself out on dates.

- Romanticize eating alone at a cute café or trying a new restaurant.
- Go on a solo adventure—a bookstore run, a museum visit, a scenic walk.
- Order yourself your **favorite meal or dessert**—because you deserve to treat yourself.

Create a self-care night.

- Run a **bubble bath, light candles, and put on your favorite playlist.**
- Do an at-home spa night—skincare, face masks, body oil, the works.
- Journal under soft lighting with a cup of tea or wine.

Write love letters to yourself.

- Acknowledge your **growth, resilience, and beauty.**
- Celebrate your wins, no matter how small.
- **Read your own words back** and realize how much love you deserve from yourself.

Dance, laugh, and be silly—even when no one's watching.

- Put on music and **move freely**—your body deserves joy.
- Laugh **at your own jokes,** be playful, and enjoy your own energy.
- Remember: **Your relationship with yourself should be fun, not just serious.**

The more you love your own energy, the less you seek outside validation.

When you become your **own best company,** you no longer:

Settle for low-quality connections out of boredom.

Attach your happiness to someone else's presence.

Feel uncomfortable being alone, because **you enjoy yourself too much.**

Exercise: What's one way you can start enjoying your own company more?

- Can you plan a solo date this week?

- Can you set up a cozy self-care ritual just for you?
- Can you write yourself a letter about how far you've come?

Main character energy means falling in love with your life, even when no one's around to watch.

5. Romanticizing the Hard Days – How to Find Beauty Even in the Chaos

Romanticizing your life doesn't mean ignoring struggles—it means finding light in them.

Let's be real: **Not every day is glamorous.** Some days, life feels heavy. Some moments feel frustrating, exhausting, or even heartbreaking. **But even in those moments, you can still choose to see the beauty in the journey.**

Main characters don't have perfect lives—they have challenges, growth arcs, and setbacks. But what makes them powerful? **They rise, they learn, they transform.**

How to Romanticize the Hard Days:

Play soft music while you clean up a mess.
- Whether it's your room, your workspace, or your emotions—**curate an environment that soothes you.**
- Light a candle, open a window, and **turn the moment into a scene, not a burden.**

Journal your feelings in a cozy setting with a warm drink.
- **Your struggles deserve to be acknowledged, not suppressed.**

- Write them out, **but from a place of reflection, not hopelessness.**
- Ask yourself: **What is this teaching me? How will I grow from this?**

Romanticize resilience.

- The "rainy day" scenes in movies always come before a breakthrough, right?
- Imagine yourself as the main character, **navigating a challenge that will only make your story more powerful.**

Take a deep breath and remind yourself: This is just one chapter of my story—it's not the whole book.

- You are evolving.
- You are learning.
- **The version of you on the other side of this will look back and see how necessary this moment was.**

Main characters go through challenges too—but they always come out stronger.

The best part? **You get to decide how this chapter shapes you.**

Are you going to let this break you, or build you? Are you going to let this moment define you, or refine you?

Exercise: How can you shift your perspective during difficult moments to see them as part of your growth journey?

- Can you remind yourself that discomfort = growth?
- Can you visualize your future self thanking you for pushing through?

- Can you create a personal ritual that helps you reset during tough times?

Romanticizing life means embracing ALL of it—the highs, the lows, and everything in between.

Final Thoughts: Your Life is a Work of Art—Start Treating it Like One

You don't need to wait for something "big" to happen to start feeling excited about your life.

- Your life **isn't on hold** until the dream job, the perfect relationship, or the "glow-up" happens.
- The magic? **It's already here.** Right now.

Every day holds beauty, magic, and meaning—you just have to start paying attention.

- The way sunlight hits your window in the morning.
- The feeling of fresh air filling your lungs.
- The laughter in a conversation. The first sip of your favorite drink.
- **These are the moments that make up a life well-lived.**

Your life is already special. It's time to start seeing it that way.

- You are the artist of your own experience.
- **You get to create the energy, the story, the vibe.**

So light the candle. Play the music. Romanticize every second.

Because **you, my love, are the main character.**

Affirmation:

"I am the main character. My life is magical, intentional, and full of beauty. I romanticize every moment."

Chapter 23: Be a Lover, Not a Hater

Let's be real—**people who truly love themselves don't have time for negativity.**

When you're secure in who you are, **you don't feel the need to compare, compete, or criticize.** You don't waste energy on jealousy or bitterness because **you're too busy creating a life you love.** Your focus isn't on what others have—**it's on what you're building for yourself.**

Loving yourself **shifts your entire mindset.** You stop seeing other people's wins as a threat because **you know your success is inevitable.** You stop entertaining drama because **your peace is too valuable to trade for petty distractions.** You move with confidence, ease, and a deep trust in yourself, knowing that **what's meant for you will never pass you by.**

Loving yourself makes you magnetic to good things.

The more you invest in yourself, the more your energy shifts.

Confidence replaces insecurity.

Gratitude replaces comparison.

Inner peace replaces the need for outside validation.

And when you focus on **what lights you up,** negativity naturally fades into the background.

Because at the end of the day? **The energy you put out is the energy you attract.**

1. How True Self-Love Makes You Naturally Magnetic

Your energy is your most powerful currency.

Have you ever met someone who just *lights up a room*? It's not because they're the most attractive, the wealthiest, or the most accomplished—it's their **energy**.

Self-love creates a natural magnetism that **pulls in opportunities, people, and experiences that align with your highest self.** It's not about being perfect. It's about having an unshakable inner glow that makes others want to be around you.

People Who Love Themselves Radiate:

Confidence – Not loud, in-your-face arrogance, but a calm, unshakable belief in themselves. They don't need validation because they already know their worth.

Peace – They move with ease because they're centered within. They don't let negativity throw them off course, and they don't waste energy on drama.

Authenticity – They don't shrink themselves or pretend to be something they're not just to fit in. They own who they are, unapologetically.

When you embody self-love, you become a magnet for everything meant for you. People gravitate toward you, opportunities seem to come effortlessly, and life starts flowing in your favor.

And on the flip side?

People who are always bitter, negative, or judgmental push good things away.

- Jealousy repels abundance.
- Insecurity blocks confidence.

- Resentment keeps you stuck.

Your vibe attracts your tribe, your opportunities, and your experiences. If you want better things in life, it starts with **loving yourself first.**

Exercise:

Think of someone whose energy *inspires* you.

- What qualities do they have that make them magnetic?
- How do they carry themselves?
- How can you embody that in your own way?

Because at the end of the day? **Your energy is your calling card. Make sure it's one that attracts everything you deserve.**

2. The Ripple Effect of Loving Yourself

When you love yourself, everything around you shifts.

Self-love isn't just about *you*—it's about how your energy influences the world around you. The way you treat yourself sets the tone for how others treat you. The way you carry yourself inspires those around you. And the way you show up for yourself creates a ripple effect that reaches far beyond what you can see.

Your relationships get healthier.

- You attract people who genuinely respect you **because you respect yourself.**
- You stop tolerating one-sided connections or draining interactions.
- You surround yourself with people who uplift you rather than bring you down.

Your mindset expands.

- You stop wasting time on insecurities and **start focusing on what actually matters.**
- Instead of worrying about what others think, you trust yourself and your decisions.
- Fear of failure fades because **you believe in your ability to handle anything.**

You start moving with purpose.

- You're no longer chasing, forcing, or proving—you're just *being*.
- You trust your path instead of constantly second-guessing yourself.
- You take action that aligns with your values rather than seeking external validation.

You become an inspiration.

- When you love yourself unapologetically, it gives others permission to do the same.
- People notice your glow and start asking, *"What's your secret?"*
- Without even trying, you encourage others to step into their own power.

Your self-love doesn't just change your life—it creates a ripple effect that touches everyone around you.

- **When you choose confidence, others feel safer to do the same.**
- **When you set boundaries, others learn to respect their own.**

- **When you operate from love, you create a world where love multiplies.**

Exercise:

How has self-love already started to change the way you interact with the world?

- Have your relationships improved?
- Do you handle challenges differently?
- Have people started treating you with more respect?

Because the more love you give to yourself, **the more you radiate it into the world.**

3. Why Loving Yourself is the Most Powerful Thing You Can Do

Loving yourself is not just a feeling—it's a decision.

It's an active choice you make every single day. It's not just about feeling good about yourself when things are going right—it's about committing to your own well-being, your own peace, and your own growth even when life feels messy.

It's waking up and choosing:

To celebrate yourself instead of criticizing yourself.

- Instead of nitpicking your flaws, you recognize your strengths.
- Instead of dwelling on what you lack, you focus on everything you bring to the table.
- You realize you are worthy of love and appreciation— *especially* from yourself.

To be at peace with where you are while striving for more.

- You stop waiting for the "perfect" version of yourself to feel confident.
- You understand that you can desire growth while still loving yourself in the present.
- You trust that you are exactly where you need to be right now.

To let go of anything that doesn't serve your highest good.

- You stop forcing relationships, situations, or mindsets that hold you back.
- You recognize that walking away isn't weakness—it's self-respect.
- You understand that what you release makes space for something better.

To move through life with confidence, ease, and trust.

- You no longer feel the need to prove yourself to anyone.
- You operate with a quiet confidence, knowing that you are enough as you are.
- You trust yourself to handle whatever comes your way.

Haters, negativity, and self-doubt lose their power when you're truly secure in yourself.

When you are rooted in self-love:

People's opinions don't shake you.

External validation is just a bonus—not something you *need*.

You don't beg for love, respect, or attention—you naturally attract it.

Because when you love yourself deeply, unapologetically, and without conditions, you step into your highest, most magnetic, most unstoppable self.

And that? That's the ultimate flex.

Final Thoughts: Love Yourself, Love Your Life

The way you treat yourself sets the tone for everything in your life.

- Your relationships, your confidence, your success—it all starts with how you see and value yourself.
- The more you love and respect yourself, the more the world reflects that back to you.

When you embody love, you attract love in all forms.

- Love isn't just about romance—it's about friendships, opportunities, experiences, and the way life flows in your favor.
- When you radiate self-love, the right people and the right situations naturally find you.

Your self-love is the foundation for the life you're meant to live.

- Every goal, every dream, every next-level version of yourself requires self-love first.
- You cannot build a fulfilling life on a foundation of self-doubt.

So, are you going to spend your energy hating, doubting, and settling?

Or are you going to:

Step into your power?

Own your worth?

Live with love and confidence?

The choice is yours. And it always has been.

Affirmation:

"I am love. I radiate confidence, peace, and authenticity. The more I love myself, the more life loves me back."

Part 5: Healing – The Heart of Self-Love

Introduction to Healing & Self-Love

What Healing Actually Means

Healing is often misunderstood. It's not about "fixing" yourself—because **you are not broken.** You were never broken. Healing isn't about erasing pain, pretending it never happened, or becoming some perfectly enlightened version of yourself.

True healing is about:

- **Understanding** your wounds, not running from them.
- **Learning** to sit with your emotions without judgment.
- **Letting go** of what no longer serves you—while keeping the lessons.
- **Choosing** self-compassion over self-criticism.
- **Embracing** your wholeness, even with the scars.

Healing doesn't mean going back to who you were before the pain—it means growing into who you were always meant to be.

Why Healing is the Foundation of Self-Love

You can't truly love yourself without healing. Think of self-love as a beautiful home—if the foundation is cracked, no matter how much you decorate it, it won't feel safe. Healing is **laying a solid foundation** so your self-love can be strong, real, and unshakable.

When we don't heal, we carry:

Limiting beliefs (*I'm not good enough, I don't deserve love*)

Emotional baggage (*fear of abandonment, resentment, unprocessed trauma*)

Self-sabotaging behaviors (*avoiding love, overworking, settling for less*)

Healing helps you clear the clutter so you can love yourself *fully*. It's the process of untangling what isn't truly *you*—and making space for the person you are meant to be.

The Messy, Non-Linear Process of Healing

Spoiler alert: **there is no "perfect" way to heal.** Healing is *not* a straight path—it's messy, emotional, and full of ups and downs. Some days you'll feel like you've conquered your past; other days, an old wound will resurface when you least expect it. And that's *okay*.

Healing looks like:

Making progress, then having setbacks.

Feeling better one day and heavy the next.

Thinking you've "moved on," only to feel triggered again.

Realizing healing isn't a destination—it's a lifelong journey.

Healing is a cycle of **awareness, acceptance, and action.** You can't rush it, force it, or skip parts. The key is to keep going, even when it feels slow. Every step—no matter how small—is a step toward freedom.

Self-Compassion: The Most Important Tool for Growth

If healing is the foundation of self-love, **self-compassion is the glue that holds it together.** You can't heal by shaming yourself into growth—you heal by loving yourself through it.

Self-compassion looks like:

- Speaking to yourself with kindness, not judgment.
- Allowing yourself to rest without guilt.
- Accepting that your past does not define your worth.
- Giving yourself permission to feel and process emotions.

Mantra: *"I am patient with myself as I heal. I honor my journey, no matter how slow or messy it may be."*

Healing isn't about becoming someone new—it's about remembering who you've always been underneath the pain. And as you move through this section, you'll learn to heal in a way that allows you to love yourself deeper than ever before.

Chapter 24: Nurturing Your Inner Child

Reconnecting with the part of you that still needs love, validation, and safety.

No matter how much you grow, achieve, or evolve—there is still a part of you that longs to be seen, heard, and cared for. That part? **Your inner child.**

Your inner child holds the first memories of joy, wonder, and playfulness—but also the wounds, fears, and unmet needs that still echo into your present life.

Ever felt triggered by something small? That's your inner child asking to be acknowledged.

Ever craved validation, even when you "logically" know your worth? That's your inner child longing to feel safe.

Ever found yourself lighting up over the simplest, most nostalgic joys? That's your inner child reminding you who you were before the world told you otherwise.

Healing isn't just about moving forward—it's about reaching back, taking your inner child's hand, and saying: *"I see you. I hear you. And I will take care of you now."*

This chapter is about nurturing the younger version of yourself who still lives within you—giving them the love, validation, and safety they've always needed. Because when you heal your inner child, **you heal every version of yourself.**

Who is Your Inner Child? Recognizing Their Presence in Your Life

Your **inner child** is *you*—the younger version of yourself that still lives within you, carrying memories, emotions, and beliefs formed in your earliest years.

They hold onto **your first experiences of joy, your deepest fears, and the parts of you that may have never been fully heard, seen, or loved the way they needed.**

Even as you grow, your inner child doesn't disappear. They whisper through your emotions, your reactions, and even the things that bring you comfort.

How to Recognize Your Inner Child Speaking:

You feel deep emotions that seem bigger than the situation.

- Ever had a moment where something small triggered an overwhelming reaction—anger, sadness, or fear?
- That's often your inner child responding, not just to the present, but to old wounds that were never fully healed.

You crave validation and reassurance, especially in relationships.

- Do you sometimes feel desperate for approval or struggle with rejection more than seems rational?
- That's your inner child looking for the love and security they once lacked.

You struggle with feelings of abandonment, rejection, or unworthiness.

- If feeling left out, ignored, or criticized hits deeper than expected, it may be because your younger self never felt truly safe or valued.
- Old wounds don't just disappear—they resurface in new ways until they're healed.

You light up when you do things you loved as a kid.

- Ever notice how certain things—playing, creating, being silly, or indulging in nostalgia—bring an unexpected sense of joy?
- That's your inner child feeling safe enough to come out and play again.

Your inner child is always there, waiting for you to listen, comfort them, and show them they are safe and loved.

The question is: **Are you ready to reconnect with them?**

Understanding How Childhood Wounds Affect Self-Love Today

The way you were treated as a child **directly influences how you love yourself now.**

If you grew up feeling unseen, unloved, or like you had to **earn** affection, those wounds don't just disappear with time. Instead, they become deeply ingrained beliefs that shape how you treat yourself and how you show up in the world.

How Childhood Wounds Manifest in Self-Love:

How You Talk to Yourself:

- **Wounded Inner Child:** "I'm not good enough." *You struggle with self-criticism and perfectionism.*

- **Healed Inner Child:** "I am worthy as I am." *You practice self-compassion and celebrate your growth.*

How You Set Boundaries:

- **Wounded Inner Child:** "If I say no, they won't love me." *You people-please and struggle to speak up for yourself.*
- **Healed Inner Child:** "My needs matter too." *You honor your energy, set boundaries, and demand respect.*

How You Handle Emotions:

- **Wounded Inner Child:** "I shouldn't feel this way." *You avoid emotions, suppress your needs, or numb your pain.*
- **Healed Inner Child:** "My feelings are valid." *You allow yourself to feel, process, and release emotions in a healthy way.*

How You View Love:

- **Wounded Inner Child:** "I have to prove I'm worthy of love." *You chase love, settle for less, or fear abandonment.*
- **Healed Inner Child:** "I deserve love simply by being me." *You accept love that feels safe, reciprocal, and fulfilling.*

Healing your inner child means recognizing these patterns and choosing to love yourself differently.

It's about shifting the way you treat yourself—no longer operating from old wounds but from **self-love, self-trust, and self-worth.**

You are no longer that child.

You are now the loving adult who can give them the safety, love, and care they always needed.

Reparenting Yourself: Giving Yourself the Love, Safety, and Encouragement You Needed

Reparenting is the process of becoming the parent you needed—whether that means being more nurturing, protective, encouraging, or patient with yourself.

For many of us, childhood may not have provided the emotional security, validation, or love we truly needed. But the beautiful thing? **You can give it to yourself now.**

Ways to Reparent Yourself:

Speak Kindly to Yourself

- Your inner dialogue matters.
- Replace self-criticism with words you wish you had heard as a child.
- Example: Instead of "I'm so stupid for making that mistake," try "I'm learning, and it's okay to not be perfect."

Create a Safe Space for Your Emotions

- Let yourself feel without judgment or shame.
- If you were taught to suppress emotions, remind yourself: *Your feelings are valid.*
- When big emotions arise, ask yourself: *What do I need right now to feel safe and comforted?*

Validate Your Needs

- You don't have to "earn" rest, love, or care.
- You are allowed to take up space, to say no, and to protect your peace.

- Give yourself permission to prioritize your well-being without guilt.

Encourage Yourself Daily

- Celebrate small wins—every step forward matters.
- Remind yourself: "I'm proud of you," "You are doing great," "You are enough."
- Treat yourself with the same patience and encouragement you would give a child learning something new.

Set Healthy Boundaries

- Your inner child deserves to feel safe.
- Protect yourself from toxic situations, unhealthy dynamics, and people who drain your energy.
- Boundaries are not rejection—they are self-respect.

A Powerful Exercise:

Imagine sitting down with your younger self.

- What would you say to them?
- How would you reassure them?
- What would you do to make them feel loved and safe?

That's how you reparent yourself. Every time you speak to yourself with love, honor your emotions, or set a boundary, you are showing your inner child the care they always deserved.

Finding Joy Again: Bringing Play, Creativity, and Fun Back Into Your Life

Healing doesn't always have to be deep emotional work—**sometimes, healing looks like playing again.**

As kids, joy came naturally. We didn't overthink it, schedule it, or feel guilty for it.

We just **did what felt good.**

Drew just because we wanted to.

Danced like no one was watching.

Spent hours outside exploring.

Sang and laughed without worrying about what people thought.

But somewhere along the way, we started believing that play was only for kids. That fun had to be "earned." That life had to be serious, productive, and practical all the time.

Reconnecting with your inner child means allowing yourself to have fun for no reason—because joy is healing, too.

Ways to Reconnect with Joy:

Do an Activity You Loved as a Kid

- Color, dance, play a game, bake something fun—*no agenda, just enjoyment.*
- Your inner child remembers what made you light up— revisit those things.

Have a "No Guilt" Day

- Let yourself relax, be silly, and enjoy life without pressure.
- No productivity, no stress—just pure, intentional joy.

Surround Yourself with What Feels Safe & Inspiring

- Nostalgic movies, childhood snacks, cozy spaces—*create an environment that sparks warmth and happiness.*

Healing isn't just about fixing wounds—it's about reclaiming the joy that was always meant to be yours.

So go ahead—**laugh louder, dance freely, and play without a reason.**

Because the happiest, most healed version of you? **They remember how to have fun.**

Exercises for Inner Child Healing

Healing your inner child is about **acknowledging their presence, giving them the love they always deserved, and allowing them to feel safe, seen, and free.**

Try these exercises to connect with and nurture your inner child:

Write a Letter to Your Inner Child

- Speak to them like you would a younger version of yourself.
- Tell them everything they needed to hear but may never have.
- **Apologize** for any self-neglect.
- **Reassure** them that they are safe now.
- **Express love and protection**—let them know they are deeply cherished.

Example:

"Dear [your name as a child], I see you. I love you. You never had to be perfect to be worthy. I'm sorry for the times I was hard on you, but I promise to take care of you now. You are safe with me."

Do Something You Loved as a Kid

- Play outside, color, dance, build something, or watch a childhood movie.
- Eat your favorite nostalgic snack or wear something that makes you feel playful.
- Let yourself enjoy the moment *without overthinking.*

Joy is healing. Play is self-care.

Inner Child Affirmations

Say these out loud, write them down, or repeat them when you need comfort:

You are safe now.

You are loved exactly as you are.

You don't have to be perfect to be worthy.

You are allowed to rest, play, and enjoy life.

I will always protect and take care of you.

Speak to yourself like you would speak to a child you love.

Your inner child has been waiting for you. **It's time to show them they are finally safe, finally seen, and finally loved.**

Final Thought

Your inner child has always been with you—waiting for you to acknowledge them, nurture them, and remind them they are safe now.

Healing your inner child isn't about fixing what's broken—it's about reconnecting with the parts of you that were never meant to be abandoned.

Every time you choose self-love over self-criticism, you heal.

Every time you let yourself rest, play, and feel joy, you heal.

Every time you set boundaries and honor your needs, you heal.

This journey doesn't happen overnight, and it doesn't have to be perfect. But every step you take brings you closer to the most whole, joyful, and self-loving version of yourself.

And that? That's the healing your inner child has been waiting for all along.

Chapter 25: Letting Go of Self-Judgment

Releasing shame, guilt, and perfectionism so you can love yourself fully.

Let's be real—**we are our own worst critics.**

We judge ourselves for our mistakes.

We hold onto guilt long after we should've forgiven ourselves.

We compare ourselves to impossible standards and wonder why we never feel "good enough."

But here's the truth: *Self-judgment is the biggest thing standing between you and true self-love.*

You don't have to be perfect to be worthy.

You don't have to carry shame from the past when you're growing every day.

You don't have to judge yourself for things you would forgive in someone else.

It's time to release the weight of guilt, shame, and self-criticism—and step into a love that accepts *all* of you, flaws and all. Because the moment you stop being at war with yourself? **That's the moment you truly start living.**

Where Self-Judgment Comes From

Self-judgment doesn't just appear out of nowhere—it's learned. From childhood to adulthood, we absorb messages from family, society, and personal experiences that shape how we see ourselves. Over time, these influences turn into **the inner critic**—that voice inside that tells us we're not doing enough, not good enough, or that we need to *earn* our worth.

But here's the thing: **self-judgment isn't your true voice—it's a collection of external voices you've internalized over time.** And if you learned it, you can unlearn it.

Where Does Self-Judgment Come From?

Family & Upbringing

Your first understanding of love, validation, and acceptance came from your environment as a child. If you were raised in a home where love felt **conditional**—only given when you were "good," performed well, or met certain expectations—you may have internalized the idea that **you are only worthy if you are perfect.**

This can manifest as:

Constant pressure to overachieve.

Feeling guilty for resting or "not doing enough."

Harsh self-criticism when you fall short of your own standards.

But here's the truth: You were always worthy of love, even when you weren't perfect. And you still are.

Societal Expectations

We live in a world that constantly tells us we need to be *more*—more successful, more attractive, more productive, more *everything*.

Social media, beauty standards, and hustle culture reinforce the belief that:

Who you are is never enough.

You have to *earn* self-worth by achieving, proving, or perfecting yourself.

If you make mistakes or struggle, you're failing instead of growing.

But who set these impossible standards? Most of them are external narratives that don't reflect what *truly* matters.

Personal Expectations

Over time, we start **setting impossible standards for ourselves** without even realizing it. We convince ourselves that we:

Should never make mistakes.

Should be further along in life.

Should have everything figured out by now.

But **who decided these rules?** More often than not, we did—based on outdated beliefs we never questioned.

What if you released the pressure? What if you let go of the "shoulds" and just allowed yourself to be?

The Toxic Cycle of Self-Criticism (And How to Break It)

Self-judgment isn't just a passing thought—it becomes a **loop** that keeps you stuck. It's like running on a treadmill but never getting anywhere. No matter how much you achieve, how hard you try, or how much you push yourself, the feeling of **"not enough"** keeps coming back.

How Self-Criticism Creates a Toxic Loop:

1. **You feel like you're not doing "enough" or not "good enough."**

You compare yourself to others, focus on your shortcomings, or tell yourself you *should* be further along.

2. **You criticize yourself harshly, thinking it will push you to improve.**

You believe that being tough on yourself is the way to get better—so you engage in self-blame, guilt, and harsh inner talk.

3. **The criticism leads to feelings of shame, anxiety, or unworthiness.**

Instead of motivating you, the pressure makes you feel like a failure. You start to associate growth with stress instead of progress.

4. **Instead of motivating you, the shame makes you feel stuck or avoidant.**

You procrastinate, overthink, or shut down because the pressure is too much. The fear of failing again keeps you from even trying.

5. **You beat yourself up for not doing better, and the cycle repeats.**

The more stuck you feel, the harsher you become on yourself. You tell yourself, *"Why can't I just do better?"*—and the cycle continues.

Why This Cycle Doesn't Work:

Many people believe that **self-criticism = self-improvement.** But in reality? **Shaming yourself into change doesn't work.**

Breaking the Cycle Starts With Self-Compassion.

Instead of criticizing yourself into growth, **encourage** yourself into growth.

Growth happens when you feel safe and supported.

Progress comes from **self-acceptance**, not self-punishment.

You don't need to be "hard" on yourself to improve—you need to be patient, kind, and consistent.

What If You Replaced Self-Criticism With Self-Kindness?

Try asking yourself:

Would I speak to a friend this way? If not, why am I speaking to myself this way?

What if I allowed mistakes to be part of the process instead of proof that I'm failing?

How can I be on my own team instead of my own worst enemy?

You don't need to fight yourself to succeed—you need to support yourself.

Because real growth? **It doesn't come from shame. It comes from love.**

Learning to Observe Your Thoughts Instead of Identifying With Them

You are NOT your thoughts.

Your thoughts are simply **mental habits**—patterns formed by years of conditioning, experiences, and outside influences. But too often, we mistake them for absolute truth.

Have you ever had a passing thought like:

"I'm not good enough."

"I always mess things up."

"I'll never get where I want to be."

And instead of questioning it, you accepted it as fact? This is where **self-judgment thrives**—when you attach your identity to fleeting, unhelpful thoughts.

But here's the truth: Thoughts are just thoughts. They are not reality. They are not who you are.

Practice Thought Awareness:

Instead of believing every negative thought, try becoming an **observer** of your mind—like watching clouds pass in the sky.

1. **Pause when a self-critical thought appears.** Example: *"I'm such a failure."*

2. **Instead of reacting emotionally, step back and observe it.** Ask yourself:

Is this thought actually true, or is it just a conditioned habit?

Would I say this to my best friend?

3. **Reframe the thought with love and self-compassion.**

Instead of: *"I always mess up."*

Say: *"I made a mistake, but that doesn't define me. I am learning and growing."*

Instead of: *"I'll never be successful."*

Say: *"I am on my own timeline, and progress is happening every day."*

Instead of: *"I don't deserve good things."*

Say: *"I am worthy of love, happiness, and success—just as I am."*

Thoughts Are Temporary—They Do Not Define You

You don't need to fight every negative thought that pops into your mind. Simply notice them, question them, and choose to **respond with love** instead of judgment.

You are not your thoughts. You are the one who chooses which ones to believe.

The Difference Between Self-Awareness and Self-Criticism

There's a fine line between self-awareness and self-criticism. Both involve noticing your flaws, mistakes, and areas for growth—but one empowers you, while the other tears you down.

Self-Awareness: Growth-Based Thinking

Self-awareness is a powerful tool. It allows you to reflect on yourself **without attacking yourself.** It's about **understanding, learning, and improving** from a place of love and self-respect.

"I could improve in this area, and I'm willing to work on it."

"I made a mistake, but I can learn from it."

"I know I struggle with this, and I have the power to change."

Self-awareness helps you move forward because it's rooted in self-compassion and progress.

Self-Criticism: Shame-Based Thinking

Self-criticism, on the other hand, is harsh and unforgiving. It's fueled by shame, guilt, and the belief that you are somehow *not enough.* Instead of helping you grow, it leaves you feeling stuck and unworthy.

"I'm such a failure. I'll never get it right."

"I always mess things up—why do I even try?"

"I'm not good enough, so I should just stop."

Self-criticism doesn't push you forward—it holds you back in cycles of self-doubt and negativity.

How to Shift from Self-Criticism to Self-Awareness:
Catch yourself when you start being overly self-critical.

Ask: "Am I being constructive or just tearing myself down?"
Reframe your inner dialogue—talk to yourself like you would a friend.

Instead of: *"I always mess up."*

Say: *"I'm learning and growing, and that's okay."*

Instead of: *"I'm not good enough."*

Say: *"I am already enough, and I'm improving every day."*

The Key Difference?
Self-awareness encourages change. Self-criticism discourages it. One makes you stronger, the other keeps you small.

So next time you catch yourself slipping into self-judgment, **pause. Breathe. Reframe.** You are not your mistakes—you are a person who is always evolving.

Exercises to Release Self-Judgment
Letting go of self-judgment isn't just about stopping negative thoughts—it's about actively replacing them with self-compassion, acceptance, and encouragement. These exercises will help you shift your inner dialogue and start treating yourself with the kindness you deserve.

Journaling: Rewrite Your Inner Critic's Voice
Your inner critic has been running the same script for years—it's time to rewrite it.

Step 1: Write down 3-5 negative thoughts you often tell yourself.

Step 2: For each one, **reframe it with kindness,** as if you were comforting a close friend.

Step 3: Read these reframed thoughts daily until they become your new internal narrative.

Example:

Inner Critic: "I'm too behind in life."

Self-Compassion: "There is no timeline for success. I am on my own path, and I trust my journey."

Inner Critic: "I always make stupid mistakes."

Self-Compassion: "Mistakes don't define me—they teach me. I am learning and improving every day."

Inner Critic: "I'm not good enough."

Self-Compassion: "I am already enough, just as I am. My worth is not up for debate."

Bonus: Go back and read your old negative self-talk. Notice how harsh it sounds? Would you say those things to someone you love? No? Then don't say them to yourself either.

Mirror Work: Speak Self-Kindness Affirmations

Looking at yourself and speaking words of love is **one of the most powerful ways to rewire self-judgment.** It might feel weird at first, but **stick with it—your mind will start believing what you say.**

Step 1: Stand in front of a mirror and look into your own eyes.

Step 2: Say these affirmations out loud (even if it feels awkward at first!):

I am enough exactly as I am.

I release the need to be perfect.

I give myself permission to grow at my own pace.

I am proud of myself for how far I've come.

I deserve love, kindness, and peace.

Step 3: Repeat daily until these words **feel true—because they are.**

Pro Tip: If certain affirmations feel hard to say, those are the ones you need the most. Keep going until they feel natural.

Letting Go of Self-Judgment is a Practice

Releasing self-judgment **won't happen overnight**, but with consistent effort, you'll start noticing the shift.

Your self-talk will become kinder.

You'll start catching self-judgment before it spirals.

You'll replace criticism with encouragement.

And most importantly—you'll finally start treating yourself with the love and grace you've always deserved.

Final Thought

You were never meant to be perfect—you were meant to be real.

True self-love isn't about meeting impossible standards or constantly proving your worth—it's about embracing yourself, exactly as you are.

You are allowed to grow without punishing yourself.

You are allowed to make mistakes without labeling yourself a failure.

You are allowed to love yourself fully, even as you evolve.

Because the more you **release self-judgment**, the more space you create for **love, joy, and freedom.**

Chapter 26: Releasing What No Longer Serves You

Shedding the people, habits, and mindsets holding you back.

Growth requires letting go. You can't step into the next version of yourself while carrying everything—and everyone—you've outgrown.

But here's the truth: **Releasing isn't easy.**

We hold onto things—whether it's toxic relationships, self-sabotaging habits, or outdated beliefs—because they feel familiar. Because we once found comfort in them. Because part of us fears what life will look like without them.

But holding onto what no longer serves you isn't safety—it's stagnation.

Every time you let go of something that no longer aligns, you make space for something better. You step closer to your highest self. You open the door for new opportunities, new peace, and new energy that truly supports your growth.

This chapter is about **releasing without fear, detaching without guilt, and trusting that what's meant for you will never require you to hold onto something that drains you.**

Understanding Attachment: Why We Hold Onto Things That Hurt Us

Letting go isn't hard because we enjoy suffering—it's hard because we're wired to seek comfort, even in things that no longer align with us.

We attach meaning to things.

A person isn't just a person—they might represent love, security, or a piece of your past. A habit isn't just a habit—it might be something that once brought relief or stability. Letting go can feel like erasing a part of yourself, even when you know it's necessary.

We fear change.

The unknown is intimidating. Even when we *know* something isn't right for us, stepping away from it means facing uncertainty. Questions creep in:

"What if I regret this?"

"What if I never find better?"

"What if I'm making a mistake?"

We get stuck in 'what could have been.'

Sometimes, we don't hold onto *what is*—we hold onto the *potential* of something. We convince ourselves that if we just try harder, wait longer, or tolerate more, things will magically shift. But the reality? **Loving potential more than reality keeps you trapped in false hope.**

The truth? Holding on to things that drain you doesn't keep you safe—it keeps you stuck.

Real healing comes from recognizing when something has run its course and trusting yourself enough to release it. You don't need to cling to things out of fear—what's meant for you will never require you to suffer to keep it.

Identifying What's Draining Your Energy

Not everything or everyone is meant to stay in your life forever. Some things were meant to teach you, help you grow, or serve a season—**but not everything is meant to be permanent.**

Take a moment to reflect: **What in your life feels heavy, draining, or misaligned?**

What's keeping you stuck instead of helping you evolve?

Relationships:

- Do you feel seen, heard, and valued, or do you constantly feel dismissed?
- Do they respect your boundaries, or do they push past them?
- Do they bring peace into your life, or are they a constant source of stress, drama, or confusion?

Habits & Behaviors:

- Does this habit genuinely add value to my life, or is it just a distraction?
- Am I doing this out of love for myself, or is this self-sabotage?
- Is this habit moving me toward my highest self, or keeping me stuck in cycles I've outgrown?

Environments:

- Does this space make me feel safe, inspired, and at peace?
- Am I holding onto things that carry old, heavy energy—objects, memories, or even clutter that no longer serve me?

- Do I feel at home in my own space, or does it feel stagnant and draining?

If something depletes you more than it nourishes you, it may be time to let it go.

Your energy is sacred. The things, people, and spaces you surround yourself with should add to your life, not take from it.

How to Release with Love (Not Bitterness)

Letting go doesn't have to be an act of anger, resentment, or regret. You don't have to burn bridges, seek revenge, or hold onto negativity to prove you're done. **True release happens when you let go with love, peace, and gratitude.**

Why Releasing with Love is Powerful:

- Bitterness keeps you emotionally tied to what hurt you.
- Resentment drains your energy and blocks new blessings.
- When you let go with love, you free yourself completely.

Steps to Release with Love:

Acknowledge the lesson – Every situation, even painful ones, has something to teach you. Instead of focusing on the loss, ask yourself: *What did this experience show me about myself? What wisdom can I take with me?*

Accept that closure comes from within – You don't need an apology, a long conversation, or the "perfect ending" to move on. Closure is a choice you make for yourself, not something someone else gives you.

Choose gratitude over resentment – Shift your focus. Instead of, *Why did this happen to me?* try, *I'm grateful for what this taught me, and I release it with peace.*

Affirm your worth – Letting go is not a loss—it's an upgrade. You're not "losing" anything; you're creating space for something better. Trust that when you release what no longer serves you, you make room for what's truly aligned with you.

Mantra for Letting Go:

"I release what no longer serves me with love. I trust that what's meant for me will stay, and what's not will leave to make space for something greater."

Let go with peace, and watch how quickly your life starts to transform.

Setting Boundaries as an Act of Self-Respect

Letting go doesn't always mean cutting something or someone off completely—it can also mean redefining how you engage with them. Setting boundaries is how you protect your energy, maintain your peace, and ensure that your relationships, habits, and environments align with your well-being.

When Letting Go Isn't an Option, Boundaries Are the Solution

People who drain you but can't be removed (family, coworkers, etc.)

You don't have to absorb their energy or be available 24/7. **Set clear limits.** Decide what behaviors you will and won't tolerate, how much access they have to you, and when you engage with them.

→ Example: *"I'm happy to talk, but I won't engage in negativity or gossip."*

Habits that no longer serve you but are hard to break Instead of trying to quit something cold turkey, **replace it with a healthier alternative.**

→ Example: If scrolling on social media drains you, replace the habit by setting a time limit or swapping it for journaling or reading.

Environments that no longer align with you

If a space (home, work, social settings) feels heavy or uninspiring, **make small shifts to reclaim it.** Cleanse your space, add things that make you feel at peace, or start exploring new spaces that align with your energy.

→ Example: Decluttering your home, surrounding yourself with uplifting people, or spending more time in places that feel inspiring.

Boundaries are not about shutting people or experiences out—they're about honoring yourself.

Mantra for Boundaries:

"I am allowed to protect my energy. I set boundaries with love, knowing that I deserve peace, respect, and alignment in all areas of my life."

Setting boundaries is not selfish—it's an act of self-respect, and the more you honor them, the more aligned your life becomes.

Exercises to Help You Release

Letting go isn't just a mindset shift—it's something you can physically practice. These exercises will help you release what no longer serves you in a tangible way.

Decluttering Exercise: Physically Remove Things That Carry Old Energy

Your space holds energy, and sometimes, the things around you keep you tied to a version of yourself that no longer exists.

Go through your space and identify objects that feel heavy, outdated, or tied to past experiences that no longer serve you.

Ask yourself: *Does this item reflect who I am becoming?* If the answer is no, let it go.

Create a cleansing ritual—whether it's donating clothes, throwing out old journals, or reorganizing your room to reflect your next chapter.

→ *Bonus Tip:* After decluttering, cleanse your space with sage, incense, or simply open the windows and let fresh air in to invite in new energy.

Write a "Goodbye" Letter to Something or Someone You're Releasing

Sometimes, closure doesn't come from others—it comes from within. Writing a letter can help you acknowledge the role something played in your life while consciously choosing to move forward.

Write to a person, habit, belief, or version of yourself that you are letting go of.

Thank it for what it taught you. Even painful experiences had lessons.

Release it with love. Write words of closure, such as:
→ *"I no longer need you. I am choosing peace, and I trust what's ahead of me."*

Choose what to do with the letter:

Keep it as a reminder of your growth.

Burn it (safely), rip it up, or bury it to symbolize release.

Letting go isn't just about loss—it's about making space for something better. Release with love, trust, and gratitude.

Final Thought

Letting go is an act of faith—it's trusting that when you release what no longer serves you, you make room for something greater.

It's choosing to believe that what's ahead is more aligned than what's behind.

It's allowing yourself to outgrow people, habits, and mindsets without guilt.

Every time you let go of something misaligned, you step closer to the life that's meant for you.

The more you release, the more space you create—for peace, joy, and true alignment.

Mantra: *"I trust that what is meant for me will always find me."*

Chapter 27: Forgiving Yourself & Others

Freeing yourself from resentment and guilt so you can move forward.

Forgiveness isn't about excusing, forgetting, or pretending something didn't hurt you. It's about **freeing yourself** from the weight of what happened.

Holding onto resentment, whether toward yourself or someone else, only keeps you trapped in the past. It drains your energy, clouds your peace, and creates a cycle of pain that doesn't serve you. **Forgiveness is not about them—it's about you.**

It's a gift you give yourself. A decision to stop carrying what no longer belongs to you. A way to reclaim your emotional freedom and create space for healing, love, and inner peace.

This chapter is about letting go of guilt, anger, and regret—not to justify the past, but to set yourself free. Because the truth is, **you deserve to move forward.**

What Forgiveness Is & What It Isn't

Let's set the record straight—**forgiveness is not about the other person.** It's not about excusing what they did, forgetting the pain, or even letting them back into your life. **It's about you.** It's about choosing peace over resentment, freeing yourself from emotional burdens, and reclaiming your power.

Too often, people resist forgiveness because they think it means saying, *"It's okay."* But true forgiveness has nothing to do with making excuses for bad behavior. Instead, it's about recognizing that holding onto pain and resentment is only hurting **you**—not them.

Forgiveness is NOT:

Saying what they did was okay. Forgiveness is not justification. You can acknowledge the harm while still choosing to release its hold over you.

Forgetting what happened. Forgetting is not healing. You don't need to erase the past—you need to process it so it no longer controls you.

Allowing toxic people to stay in your life. You can forgive someone and still set **firm boundaries** to protect your peace.

Dropping your guard and pretending nothing happened. Forgiveness is about inner peace, not about tolerating mistreatment.

Forgiveness IS:

Releasing the emotional baggage that keeps you stuck. Holding onto resentment won't change the past—it only drains your present.

Choosing peace over anger, even when you have every reason to stay mad. You deserve to feel free.

Accepting that you cannot rewrite the past, but you can shape your future. Healing begins when you stop replaying the hurt.

Taking back your power. When you refuse to let bitterness take up space in your heart, you reclaim your energy for things that actually serve you.

Forgiveness is For You, Not for Them

It's important to understand that **you don't have to tell someone you forgive them.** You don't need to wait for an apology. You don't need to let them back in.

Forgiveness is a silent, personal act of self-liberation. It's about **releasing their grip on your emotions so you can move forward.**

A Reminder:

Holding onto anger may feel like self-protection, but it's actually **self-imprisonment.** Carrying resentment is like drinking poison and expecting the other person to suffer.

Mantra: *"I forgive, not because they deserve it, but because I deserve peace."*

Why Forgiveness is For You, Not Them

Holding onto resentment doesn't punish the other person—it **punishes you.** The truth is, while you're replaying the hurt, they might not even be thinking about it. They may have moved on, continued living their life, or never even acknowledged the pain they caused. Meanwhile, **you're still carrying the weight of it.**

The Ice Cube Analogy

Think of anger and resentment like holding an **ice cube** in your hand. At first, it might feel manageable, even justified. But the longer you grip it, the more painful it becomes. Eventually, your fingers start burning, numbing, and hurting—but the ice cube stays the same.

The pain is no longer about the ice—it's about the fact that you refuse to let it go.

This is what happens when you hold onto resentment. It doesn't hurt **them**—it keeps **you** in pain.

Forgiving Doesn't Mean They Deserve It—It Means YOU Deserve Peace

Forgiveness isn't about making excuses for someone's actions. It's not about saying, *"It's fine."* It's about saying, *"I refuse to let this control my emotions any longer."*

When you forgive, you take back your power.
You free yourself from emotional baggage.
You stop giving them space in your mind and heart.
Because the truth is—why should someone who hurt you still have control over your energy?

Forgiveness is a Power Move

Forgiving doesn't mean:
They're off the hook.
You forget what happened.
You have to let them back in.

Forgiving does mean:
You are choosing peace over pain.
You are no longer emotionally tied to that situation.
You are setting yourself free.
At the end of the day, **forgiveness isn't about them.**

It's about **you**—choosing to move forward, choosing to be free, and choosing to no longer let past pain define your future.

Letting Go of Guilt & Giving Yourself Permission to Move On

Guilt is **one of the heaviest emotions** to carry. It lingers in the back of your mind, whispering *"You should have known better."* It replays past mistakes, making you relive moments you can't change. But the truth?

You did the best you could with the knowledge, awareness, and emotional capacity you had at the time.

Think about that for a second. If you knew better, you **would** have done better. Hindsight is always clearer, but punishing yourself for a version of you that didn't have that insight yet? That's unfair.

Why Holding Onto Guilt Keeps You Stuck

Guilt tricks you into believing that if you just **feel bad enough**, you'll somehow make things right. But guilt doesn't fix the past. It doesn't undo mistakes. **It only keeps you stuck.**

Guilt doesn't change what happened.

It doesn't make you a better person.

It doesn't bring healing—it keeps you from it.

At some point, you have to ask yourself: *Am I holding onto this guilt because I need to, or because I don't know how to let it go?*

How to Release Guilt & Move Forward

Forgiving yourself doesn't mean ignoring your mistakes—it means taking accountability **without** self-punishment.

Acknowledge it.

Instead of pushing guilt down or pretending it doesn't exist, face it:

"I made a mistake, and I own it."

Learn from it.

Every mistake holds a lesson. Reflect on what you've learned so you don't repeat it:

"I now understand what I could have done differently."

Choose to move forward.

Growth means allowing yourself to evolve past the mistake instead of being defined by it:

"I will not punish myself forever—I deserve to grow."

You are human. You are allowed to make mistakes. You are allowed to evolve.

Mantra for Self-Forgiveness:

"I give myself permission to let go of guilt and embrace growth. I am worthy of peace and healing."

The past has already happened. What matters now is **what you do next.**

Self-Forgiveness: Releasing Regret & Embracing Self-Acceptance

Forgiving yourself is often **so much harder** than forgiving others. Why? Because we tend to hold ourselves to **impossible standards**—expecting to never mess up, never make the wrong choice, never fail.

But self-love requires self-forgiveness.

You are **not** meant to go through life without mistakes. Mistakes are how you learn, how you grow, how you evolve. Holding onto regret won't undo the past—it only keeps you from living fully in the present.

The Heavy Weight of Regret

"I should have known better."

"I can't believe I let that happen."

"I wish I could go back and do things differently."

We replay these thoughts like a **broken record**, as if punishing ourselves will somehow change the past. But ask yourself:

Is holding onto this regret helping me become better, or is it just keeping me stuck?

The truth is, **regret is only useful if it teaches you something.** Beyond that, it's just emotional self-harm.

Speaking to Yourself with Compassion

Imagine your **younger self** standing in front of you. Would you speak to them the way you speak to yourself now?

Would you shame them for what they didn't know yet? Would you tell them they're unworthy because they made a mistake? Would you say, *"You should have been perfect"*?

Of course not. You'd probably hug them and say, *"You did your best with what you knew at the time. And I love you anyway."*

So why not extend that same grace to yourself now?

Forgiveness is Self-Love

Forgiveness is self-acceptance. It's recognizing that you are more than your mistakes.

Forgiveness is healing. It allows you to release pain and move forward.

Forgiveness is freedom. It lets you break free from the chains of the past.

You are worthy of self-forgiveness. You always have been.

Mantra for Self-Forgiveness:

"I am allowed to grow. I am allowed to evolve. I am allowed to forgive myself and move forward in love."

Daily Forgiveness Affirmations (For When You're Struggling to Let Go)

Sometimes, you need daily reminders that you are healing and releasing. Repeat these affirmations whenever you feel resentment creeping back in:

"Forgiveness is a gift I give myself."

"I choose to free myself from the weight of the past."

"I release this pain because I deserve peace."

"I forgive, not because they deserve it, but because I do."

"I allow myself to move forward with love and strength."

Forgiveness is not a one-time event—it's a practice. Be patient with yourself as you heal.

Final Thought: You Deserve to Be Free

You are not defined by what happened to you, and you are not defined by your mistakes. You are more than the pain you've carried, more than the moments that hurt you, and more than the choices you wish you could redo.

Forgiveness is not about erasing the past—it's about releasing its hold on you.

When you hold onto resentment, guilt, or regret, it's like carrying a heavy weight that was never meant to be yours forever. But the moment you choose to forgive, you begin to set yourself free.

Forgiving others doesn't mean you excuse what they did—it means you're no longer allowing their actions to take space in your heart.

Forgiving yourself doesn't mean you ignore your mistakes—it means you accept your humanity, learn, and allow yourself to grow.

You don't have to keep punishing yourself. You don't have to stay tied to the hurt. You deserve peace. You deserve healing. You deserve love, especially from yourself.

Let go—not for them, but for you. Because the moment you release the weight of the past, you open yourself up to the freedom, joy, and love that was always meant for you.

Mantra: *"I choose peace. I release resentment. I forgive myself. I am free."*

Chapter 28: Emotional Alchemy

Transforming pain into power and learning to process emotions in a healthy way.

Emotions are energy—they are meant to move through you, not control you. Yet, so many people either suppress their feelings or let them consume them. But what if, instead of fearing or avoiding emotions, you learned to **work with them**?

Emotional alchemy is the art of turning emotional pain into growth, strength, and wisdom. It's about recognizing that every emotion—no matter how difficult—holds a message, a lesson, and an opportunity for transformation.

When you master emotional alchemy, you no longer feel trapped by sadness, anger, or fear. Instead, you learn how to **process, release, and transform** those emotions into something that serves you.

This chapter is about learning how to sit with your feelings without drowning in them, how to channel your emotions into self-growth, and how to take control of your inner world so that no outside force can shake your peace. Because true power isn't about never feeling pain—it's about knowing how to **turn pain into power.**

Why Suppressing Emotions Keeps You Stuck

We live in a world that often glorifies emotional suppression. From childhood, we're conditioned to "stay strong," "shake it off," or "keep pushing forward" without fully addressing what we feel. But **pushing emotions down doesn't make them disappear—it only** buries them deeper, where they silently shape our behaviors, beliefs, and self-worth.

Unprocessed emotions don't just vanish; they resurface in unexpected ways.

When you suppress emotions instead of working through them, they manifest in ways you may not immediately recognize:

Anxiety – When fear, stress, or uncertainty is left unacknowledged, it lingers beneath the surface, creating restlessness, racing thoughts, and constant worry.

Anger & Resentment – When past hurt isn't processed, it turns into bitterness, causing you to lash out, become defensive, or carry unresolved grudges.

Fatigue & Burnout – Carrying emotional weight without release can leave you feeling physically and mentally exhausted, even when you're doing "nothing."

Self-Sabotage – Unhealed wounds can lead to destructive patterns, like procrastination, unhealthy coping mechanisms, or pushing people away when they get too close.

You can't heal what you don't allow yourself to feel. Suppression is like stuffing down an overflowing suitcase— eventually, it bursts open. **The only way out is through.**

Healing begins when you **allow yourself to sit with your emotions instead of running from them**—to process what's truly beneath the surface and release it in a way that **serves you instead of controls you.**

Learning to Sit with Emotions Instead of Running from Them

Most people avoid emotions, not because they don't feel them, but because they're afraid of what they might uncover. We distract ourselves with work, social media, food, or unhealthy habits— anything to escape the discomfort. But **emotions aren't your enemy—they're messengers trying to tell you something.** The more you suppress them, the louder they become.

Instead of running from emotions, try **leaning into them** with curiosity and compassion. Here's how:

The Next Time an Uncomfortable Emotion Comes Up, Try This:

1. Pause & Acknowledge

Before reaching for a distraction, stop and name what you're feeling.

Example: "I feel sad right now," or "I feel anxious and don't know why."

Why? Naming emotions reduces their intensity. It shifts you from *reacting* to *observing*.

2. Observe Without Judgment

Instead of labeling emotions as "good" or "bad," just notice them.

Example: "This feeling is present, but it does not define me."

Why? When you remove judgment, emotions lose their power over you.

3. Ask What It's Teaching You

Emotions carry wisdom. Ask yourself: *What does this feeling need?*

Comfort? (Maybe you need rest or self-care.)

- Understanding? (Is this emotion tied to an old wound?)
- Release? (Do you need to express it through movement, writing, or talking?)

  Why? Every emotion serves a purpose—it either highlights something unhealed or helps you process a current experience.

4. Allow It to Move Through You

Emotions are energy, and when you resist them, they get trapped.

Instead of suppressing:

Breathe – Take slow, deep breaths to regulate your nervous system.

Move – Stretch, dance, or go for a walk to physically release emotional tension.

Express – Write it out, cry if you need to, or talk to someone you trust.

Why? The more you allow emotions to flow, the quicker they pass. Suppression = suffering. Processing = peace.

Mantra:

"I allow myself to feel, process, and release with love."

The goal isn't to "fix" emotions—it's to create space for them. The more you sit with your feelings instead of running, the more emotionally free and powerful you become.

Healthy Ways to Express & Release Emotions

Emotions are meant to be experienced, not bottled up. When you allow yourself to express and release emotions in healthy ways, you free up space for healing and growth. **It's not about acting on every emotion; it's about feeling them and letting them flow.** Here's how to express and release emotions in a way that honors your emotional landscape:

Crying

Crying isn't a sign of weakness; it's a powerful release mechanism. When we hold in our tears, emotions like sadness, frustration, or even joy can become trapped in the body. **Let yourself cry without guilt.**

Why? Crying helps to release emotional tension and brings relief. It clears your emotional field so you can move forward.

Journaling

When emotions are overwhelming, put pen to paper. Writing freely without editing your thoughts allows you to release pent-up feelings and gain insight into what's really going on.

Why? Journaling gives you the space to process emotions without judgment. It helps to untangle complicated feelings and offers clarity.

Movement

Our bodies store emotions. Have you ever felt your shoulders tense up during a stressful situation? **Movement helps to release that tension.** Whether it's dancing, stretching, yoga, or even going for a walk, movement gets the emotional energy flowing.

Why? Physical movement helps to ground you and releases built-up emotional energy, promoting a sense of calm and relief.

Breathwork & Meditation

When emotions are intense, your breath can be the anchor that keeps you calm. **Deep breathing** activates the parasympathetic nervous system, reducing stress and promoting emotional balance. Meditation helps center your thoughts, allowing you to sit with your emotions without being overwhelmed by them.

Why? Breathwork and meditation create space for emotions to pass through your body with clarity and calmness.

Artistic Expression

Channel your emotions into creative outlets like painting, drawing, writing poetry, or even crafting. When words aren't enough, art can help express what's inside.

Why? Creative expression taps into your subconscious, allowing you to express emotions in a non-verbal way. It can also be deeply cathartic and healing.

The Goal

The goal isn't to suppress emotions but to move them through your body in a way that feels safe and freeing. It's about **feeling the feelings** and then **letting them go**—creating emotional flow so you can embrace the next moment with openness and clarity.

Turning Pain into Wisdom: Seeing Hardships as Teachers, Not Punishments

Pain is an inevitable part of life, but it doesn't have to define us. In fact, **pain can be one of our greatest teachers**—if we're open to the lessons it holds. **The challenge lies in shifting our mindset** to view our struggles as opportunities for growth instead of roadblocks.

Shift Your Perspective

Instead of asking, *"Why did this happen to me?"* ask yourself, *"What is this teaching me?"*

Every hardship carries valuable wisdom:

- **Heartbreak?** It teaches you your **self-worth**—showing you what you will and won't tolerate in love.
- **Failure?** It teaches **resilience**—helping you realize that setbacks aren't the end, but part of the process of growth.
- **Loss?** It teaches you to **appreciate the present**—reminding you that nothing is promised and every moment counts.
- **Struggles?** They build your **strength**—showing you how much you can endure and how much growth is possible through difficulty.

When you reframe pain as a tool for personal evolution, it transforms from something to avoid to something to embrace. Each struggle shapes you into a stronger, wiser version of yourself. **Instead of feeling punished, you begin to see pain as a catalyst for your growth.**

Mantra: *"I trust that even my pain has purpose."*

When you trust that every hardship is meant to teach you something valuable, you reclaim your power. Pain no longer holds you captive; it becomes a stepping stone on your path to becoming the best version of yourself.

Exercises for Emotional Alchemy

Emotional Check-In: Learning to Name & Understand Your Feelings

Start by tuning into your emotional state with a simple self-check-in.

1. **Ask yourself:** *What am I feeling right now?* Recognizing and naming emotions is the first step to releasing them.

2. **Identify where you feel it in your body:** Does it feel like a tight chest? Heavy shoulders? A knot in your stomach? Understanding the physical manifestation of your emotions can help you address them with care.

3. **Ask yourself:** *What does this emotion need from me?* Does it need expression through journaling? Rest through self-care? Reassurance from within? Once you understand the need, provide that to yourself.

Why It Helps:

Naming your emotions helps you separate yourself from them, allowing you to process them instead of being overwhelmed or consumed. When you acknowledge and understand your emotions, you create space for release and healing.

Movement Exercise: Using Dance, Stretching, or Shaking to Release Emotions

Let's use your body as a vessel to release what your mind holds onto. Emotions are energy, and energy must move to be processed.

1. **Choose music** that reflects the emotion you're experiencing.
   Whether it's a soft, reflective tune or an upbeat, intense anthem, let the music reflect what you're feeling.

2. **Let your body move freely**—don't overthink it. Shake, sway, jump, or stretch—let your body move in the way it naturally wants to.

3. **Release with intention.**
   Allow any pent-up energy, frustration, or sadness to flow out as you move. Don't try to control it; let it go with every movement.

Why It Helps:

Moving your body helps break the emotional blockages that can form when emotions stay stuck. Dance, shaking, and stretching help release tension and bring emotions back into flow, allowing them to leave the body instead of remaining trapped.

Final Thought:

Emotions are not your enemy. They are your guides, offering valuable insight into your inner world. When you learn to sit with them, express them, and transform them, you unlock a deeper understanding of yourself and your needs. By embracing emotional freedom, you create space for healing, growth, and unconditional self-love. This process is not just about processing emotions—it's about reclaiming your power and living with intention, peace, and authenticity.

Mantra: *"I embrace my emotions, knowing they are here to guide and empower me."*

Chapter 29: Reclaiming Your Power

Owning your story, setting standards, and stepping into your highest self.

Power isn't something anyone gives you—it's something you claim. Reclaiming your power means owning your past without shame, standing firm in your worth, and refusing to settle for less than you deserve. It's about rewriting your narrative, setting unapologetic standards, and walking with the confidence of someone who knows exactly who they are.

This chapter is about stepping into your highest self—not just in the way you move through the world, but in how you think, speak, and make choices. It's about no longer dimming your light for others' comfort, but shining so brightly that you illuminate your own path forward. When you truly reclaim your power, you stop waiting for permission to live the life you desire—you create it. And the best part? Once you embrace this version of yourself, there's no going back.

Understanding That Healing Doesn't Mean Erasing the Past—It Means Reclaiming It

For so long, you may have wanted to erase certain parts of your past—the pain, the mistakes, the moments where you felt powerless. Maybe you wished you could go back in time and rewrite the story, make different choices, or avoid certain experiences altogether. But true healing isn't about deleting those experiences. It's about owning them.

Healing is not about pretending the past never happened or burying it so deep that you never have to look at it again. That's not freedom—that's avoidance. And avoidance only gives your past more control over you. The real power comes when you reclaim those moments and shift how they exist within you.

Your past doesn't define you, but it has shaped you. Every hardship, every lesson, every challenge has contributed to the person you are becoming. Strength isn't built in comfort—it's built in resilience. The moments that broke you also built you. The experiences that hurt you also taught you. The versions of yourself that struggled were still *you*, doing the best you could with what you knew at the time. And now, with growth and wisdom, you get to decide how your story moves forward.

Instead of seeing your past as something to be ashamed of, see it as your proof of resilience. You are not the things that happened to you. You are the person who *survived* them. You are the person who took pain and turned it into wisdom, who turned losses into lessons, and who is now stepping into their highest self—not in spite of the past, but because of it.

Mantra: *"My past is not a burden—it is my strength."*

Breaking Free from Victim Mentality: You Are Not What Happened to You!

There is a difference between acknowledging your pain and living in it.

Yes, people have hurt you. Yes, life has been unfair at times. Yes, you didn't deserve certain things that happened. But what you do from this point forward is your choice. Holding onto a victim mindset only keeps you trapped in the very thing you want to escape.

Your pain is valid. Your struggles are real. But staying stuck in the narrative of "this happened to me, so I can't move forward" only gives more power to the things that broke you. Reclaiming your power means deciding that your pain does not get to dictate your future—you do.

It's easy to get caught in cycles of resentment, anger, or self-pity. But at some point, you have to ask yourself: *Do I want to be right about how unfair life has been, or do I want to be free?* Because real freedom begins when you stop seeing yourself as powerless and start recognizing your ability to change the story.

Reclaiming your power means shifting your mindset from:
"Why did this happen to me?" → *"What did this teach me?"*
"I have no control." → *"I get to decide how I move forward."*
"I'll never be happy." → *"I have the power to create the life I deserve."*

Your past does not define your future. You do. You are not what happened to you—you are what you choose to become.

Mantra: *"I am not a victim of my past—I am the author of my future."*

Learning to Trust Yourself Again: Self-Trust is the Foundation of Self-Love

One of the biggest parts of reclaiming your power is learning to trust yourself. If you've been through pain, betrayal, or self-doubt, you may have stopped listening to your own intuition. Maybe you've made choices in the past that didn't turn out the way you hoped, and now you hesitate before making decisions. Maybe someone made you feel like you couldn't trust your own judgment, so you started looking to others for validation. But here's the truth—nobody knows you better than *you*.

When you don't trust yourself, life feels uncertain. You second-guess every decision, you seek approval before taking action, and you feel disconnected from your own wants and needs. Rebuilding self-trust isn't about getting everything right all the time—it's about believing in your ability to handle whatever comes your way.

Signs You Need to Rebuild Self-Trust:

- **You constantly second-guess yourself.**
  You replay decisions in your head, overanalyzing every possible outcome. Even when you make a choice, you question if it was the right one, leaving you in a cycle of self-doubt.

- **You rely on others to validate your decisions.**
  Instead of trusting your own instincts, you look to others for approval before making a move. You feel uneasy making choices alone and seek reassurance before believing in yourself.

- **You feel disconnected from your own wants and needs.**
  You struggle to identify what truly makes you happy or fulfilled. You've spent so much time prioritizing others' opinions or expectations that your own desires feel unclear or out of reach.

- **You hesitate to take action out of fear of making the "wrong" choice.**
  Instead of trusting yourself to figure things out, you become paralyzed by indecision. You'd rather not choose at all than risk choosing "wrong," even though not deciding is a decision in itself.

- **You ignore your intuition, even when something doesn't feel right.**
  You've felt that inner nudge before—the subtle knowing that something is off or that a certain path is meant for you. But instead of trusting it, you push it aside, convincing yourself that logic, external opinions, or fear should take priority.

Recognizing these signs is the first step. The next? Rebuilding that trust—one choice, one moment, one promise to yourself at a time.

How to Rebuild Self-Trust

Keep promises to yourself – Even small ones. If you say you're going to rest, rest. If you say you'll start something, start. The more you follow through on your own word, the more you reinforce the belief that you can rely on yourself. Self-trust isn't about perfection—it's about consistency.

Listen to your intuition – That gut feeling you get? It's there for a reason. If something doesn't feel right, trust that feeling. If something excites you, explore it. Your intuition is like an internal GPS—one that works best when you stop ignoring it and start tuning in.

Celebrate your decisions – Even if they don't always work out perfectly, acknowledge your ability to choose for yourself. Every decision you make is a step forward, whether it leads to success or a lesson. The more you trust your judgment, the stronger it becomes.

Stop seeking permission – You don't need external validation to make choices about your own life. Seeking constant reassurance from others weakens your confidence in yourself. Trust that *you* know what's best for *you*.

Forgive yourself for past mistakes – Self-trust weakens when you hold onto regret or shame. But mistakes don't define you—they teach you. Instead of using past choices as reasons to doubt yourself, use them as proof that you are always learning and growing.

Rebuilding self-trust takes time, but it's worth it. Because once you trust yourself again, you no longer need constant reassurance. You no longer feel lost. You become your own source of guidance, confidence, and strength. And that is where real power begins.

Mantra: *"I trust myself. I am capable. I know what is best for me."*

Setting Standards for How You Allow Yourself to Be Treated

Reclaiming your power means raising your standards—not just for others, but for *yourself.* The way people treat you is often a reflection of what you allow. When you have strong standards, you stop tolerating what doesn't serve you, and you naturally attract better experiences, relationships, and opportunities.

Many people confuse **standards** with **boundaries**, but they are not the same.

Standards vs. Boundaries:

- **Standards** = What you expect from life (how people treat you, how you treat yourself).
- **Boundaries** = The rules you enforce to protect those standards.

For example, if your standard is that you deserve respectful and healthy communication, your boundary is refusing to engage in toxic conversations or shutting down disrespectful behavior. Standards define what you accept; boundaries ensure you don't accept anything less.

Examples of Power Standards:

I do not entertain people who drain me. – If someone constantly takes from me without giving, I remove myself.

I do not overextend myself to prove my worth. – My value is not measured by how much I do for others.

I do not settle for relationships that feel one-sided. – I give and receive love in balance, not at my own expense.

I do not dim my light to make others comfortable. – My success, joy, and confidence are not up for negotiation.

When you set standards and follow through on them, you show yourself and the world that you are serious about your worth. You no longer accept breadcrumbs when you deserve the whole feast.

Mantra: *"I only allow what aligns with my highest self."*

Exercises to Reclaim Your Power

Reclaiming your power is an active process—it's about making choices, shifting your mindset, and stepping into your highest self with confidence. These exercises will help you break old patterns, set strong intentions, and start living in alignment with your worth.

Write a Manifesto: Declare Who You Are & What You Deserve

A manifesto is a bold, unapologetic statement of who you are and what you will no longer tolerate. This is your declaration to yourself and the world about the energy you will accept and the standards you will uphold.

Example Manifesto:

"I am strong. I am worthy. I am in control of my life. I no longer entertain what drains me, disrespects me, or diminishes me. I choose peace, confidence, and alignment with my highest self. I am stepping into my power, and I make no apologies for it."

Action Step: Write your own personal manifesto. Read it daily. Speak it out loud. Let it be a reminder of the power you hold.

Confidence-Building Challenge: Do One Thing Daily That Makes You Feel Powerful

Confidence isn't something you wait for—it's something you *build* through action. The more you show up for yourself, the more powerful you will feel. Each day, challenge yourself to do one thing that affirms your strength, self-worth, and authority over your life.

Some ideas:

Speak up for yourself in a situation where you'd normally stay quiet.

- Wear something that makes you feel bold and confident.
- Set (and enforce) a boundary with someone.
- Do something outside your comfort zone (even if it's small).
- Make a decision without asking for anyone's opinion.
- Start a habit that benefits *you* (without guilt).

Every time you take a step toward reclaiming your power, you reinforce the truth that *you* are in control of your life.

Reminder: *Confidence is built through action. The more you show up for yourself, the more powerful you will feel.*

Final Thought

Your power was never lost—you just needed to reclaim it.

You are not a product of your past. You are not defined by what happened to you. You are a force of strength, resilience, and self-love. Every challenge you've faced has only made you stronger. Every lesson you've learned has shaped the person you are becoming.

Reclaiming your power is not about becoming someone new—it's about returning to the most authentic, unstoppable version of yourself. It's about knowing your worth, standing firm in your truth, and refusing to shrink for anyone.

Own your story. Set your standards. Walk into every room as the highest version of yourself, *unapologetically.*

Reminder: *You were always powerful. Now, it's time to live like it.*

Mantra: *"I am powerful. I am worthy. I am in control of my life."*

The 7-Day Self-Love Reset – A Challenge to Fully Step Into Your Power

This is it. **Everything you've learned in this book? It's time to apply it.**

This **7-day self-love reset** is designed to help you break old patterns, create new habits, and fully step into your power.

The 7-Day Self-Love Reset Plan

Day 1: Energy Detox

Remove negative energy—unfollow toxic social media, clean your space, and set boundaries.

Day 2: Affirmation Activation

Write down 5 affirmations that reflect the person you're becoming. Say them out loud in the mirror.

Day 3: Treat Yourself Like You Would Treat Someone You Love

Speak kindly to yourself, nourish your body, and do something that makes you feel good.

Day 4: Step Into Your Main Character Energy

Dress up, walk with confidence, and romanticize your routine—live like you're in the best movie ever.

Day 5: Set One Bold Boundary

Whether it's saying "no" to something draining or choosing yourself over guilt—protect your peace today.

Day 6: Move From Abundance, Not Scarcity

Make a decision today from a place of self-worth—stop acting like you're not the prize.

Day 7: Full Self-Love Reflection

Write about how you feel after this reset. What's shifted? What will you carry forward?

By the end of this week, you will feel stronger, clearer, and more in love with yourself than ever.

Journal Prompt: What was the biggest shift you experienced during this reset?

Daily Self-Love Reset Routine

A flexible, customizable guide to integrate self-love into your daily life

This is not a rigid plan—it's a guide.

Self-love isn't about forcing yourself into strict routines that feel overwhelming or unrealistic. It's about creating a rhythm of care, kindness, and intentionality that feels natural to *you*. It's about making small, meaningful choices every day that reinforce your worth, honor your needs, and nurture your well-being.

This **Self-Love Reset Routine** is designed to be **adaptable**, allowing you to build self-care into your life in a way that feels sustainable. Whether you're in a season of deep healing or simply looking for ways to reconnect with yourself, this guide will help you realign with love, balance, and inner peace.

How to Use This Routine:

Choose what speaks to you.

Adjust as needed—there's no "right" way to do it.

Let it evolve with you and your needs.

This is *your* self-love journey—make it yours.

Morning Reflection: Start the Day with Intention

How you start your morning **sets the tone** for the rest of your day. Instead of jumping straight into stress, distractions, or negativity, take a moment to center yourself and align with love and purpose.

This isn't about having a *perfect* morning routine—it's about **choosing** small, intentional moments that bring you back to yourself before the world starts pulling you in different directions.

Choose One or More Morning Practices:

Affirmations – Speak or write a self-love affirmation to set your mindset for the day.

Example: "I am worthy. I am enough. I am stepping into my power."

Gratitude – List three things you're grateful for, including one about yourself. Gratitude shifts your focus from lack to abundance.

Example: "I am grateful for my resilience. I am grateful for my body. I am grateful for another day to grow."

Breathwork/Meditation – Take 3-5 minutes to focus on your breath, set an intention, or simply sit in stillness. Even a few deep breaths can ground you in the present moment.

Movement – Stretch, dance, go for a short walk, or do anything that helps you connect with your body. Movement wakes up your energy and reminds you of your strength.

Your mornings don't have to be complicated. Just one small act of self-love can shift your entire day.

Mantra: *"I choose to start my day with love, gratitude, and intention."*

Midday Check-In: Honor Your Needs

As the day goes on, it's easy to disconnect from ourselves. **Stress, responsibilities, and external pressures** can pull us away from our self-love practices, leaving us feeling drained or out of alignment.

That's why a **midday pause** is so important. Taking just a few moments to check in with yourself can help you **reset, realign, and reconnect** with your needs.

Take a Midday Pause & Ask Yourself:

How am I feeling right now? (Tired, energized, anxious, joyful?)

Am I honoring my needs? (Have I eaten? Taken a break? Set boundaries?)

What can I do in this moment to show myself love? (Breathe, stretch, drink water, say no, say yes?)

Quick Midday Self-Love Practices:

Take a Break – Step away from work, social media, or stress for a few minutes. Breathe. Recharge.

Move Your Body – Stand up, stretch, take a short walk, shake off any tension you're holding.

Hydrate & Nourish – Drink water, eat something nourishing, and check in with your body's needs.

Reaffirm Your Worth – Say an affirmation, write a kind message to yourself, or revisit a goal you're working toward.

You deserve moments of **pause and care** throughout the day. Checking in with yourself is not selfish—it's self-respect.

Mantra: *"I check in with myself because my well-being matters."*

Evening Gratitude: End the Day with Self-Love

Your evening routine is a time to **reflect, release, and recharge**. Instead of ending the day with stress, overthinking, or scrolling endlessly on your phone, create a **peaceful, self-honoring ritual** that allows you to wind down with love.

This is your moment to appreciate yourself, let go of anything heavy, and give yourself the rest you *deserve*.

Choose One or More Evening Practices:

Gratitude Reflection – Write down or say three things you appreciate about yourself or your day. Ending the day with gratitude shifts your focus from what went wrong to what went *right*.

Example: "I am proud of myself for showing up today. I handled a challenge with grace. I honored my boundaries."

Self-Care Ritual – Take a bath, do your skincare, read, stretch, or listen to music that soothes your soul. Prioritizing rest and relaxation is an act of self-love.

Emotional Release – Journal about any lingering thoughts, worries, or emotions you need to let go of. Release anything that no longer serves you, so you don't carry it into tomorrow.

Mindful Breathing – Take a few deep breaths or do a short meditation to **signal to your body that it's safe to rest.** Even 2 minutes of deep breathing can calm your nervous system and help you sleep more peacefully.

Why This Matters:

Ending the day with **self-love and intention** allows you to go to bed feeling peaceful, rather than overwhelmed. The way you **close your day** sets the energy for the next one—so choose love, choose gratitude, choose *you*.

Mantra: *"I release the day with love. I am proud of myself. I rest with peace."*

Before Bed Self-Love Routine: Ending the Day with Peace & Gratitude

Your **before-bed routine** is a sacred time to **unwind, reflect, and connect**—with yourself, your emotions, and your higher power if that's part of your practice. Instead of carrying stress, overthinking, or tension into sleep, this routine helps you **release, reset, and rest peacefully** so you wake up feeling refreshed and aligned.

This is your invitation to **slow down, be present, and nourish yourself** before you close your eyes.

Choose Your Before-Bed Rituals:

1. Gentle Wind-Down (Relax Your Mind & Body)

Dim the lights or light a candle to create a soothing atmosphere. Play soft music, nature sounds, or enjoy silence.

Do a **gentle stretch** or take a few deep breaths to release tension from your body.

2. Gratitude & Reflection (End on a Positive Note)

Write or say three things you're grateful for—especially something about yourself.

Example: "I am grateful for my growth. I am grateful for today's lessons. I am grateful for another day of life."

Reflect on your day with kindness. Instead of focusing on what went wrong, ask:

- *What is one thing I did well today?*
- *How did I show up for myself?*
- *What lesson did today teach me?*

3. Emotional & Spiritual Release (Clear Your Mind Before Sleep)

Journal about any lingering thoughts, worries, or emotions you want to release.

Pray—speak from your heart, express gratitude, ask for guidance, or simply surrender your worries.

Visualize **letting go** of any stress, negativity, or doubts as you breathe deeply.

4. Self-Care & Comfort (Nourish Yourself Before Rest)

Do your **skincare or body care** with love—treat it as a ritual of self-care.

Make yourself a **relaxing tea** (like chamomile or lavender) if it helps you wind down.

Get cozy in **comfortable pajamas and soft blankets.**

5. Bedtime Affirmation & Breathwork (Prepare for Deep Rest)

Say a **before-sleep affirmation** to ground yourself:

"I release the day with love. I am proud of myself. I rest with peace."

Take a few **slow, deep breaths** and set an intention for peaceful, restorative sleep.

Bonus: If you like, read a few pages of a book, listen to a calming podcast, or visualize a peaceful moment before falling asleep.

Mantra: *"I surrender to rest. My mind, body, and soul are safe, loved, and at peace."*

This routine is **yours**—adjust it, make it meaningful, and allow it to be a nightly ritual of love, gratitude, and renewal.

Customizing Your Self-Love Reset Routine

This routine is **not a checklist**—it's a guide. Everything here is just an *example* of what you *could* do. You don't have to do everything. You don't even have to do the same things every day.

The most important thing? **Do what makes you feel good about you.**

Self-love is deeply personal. Some days, you might feel like doing more. Other days, you might keep it simple. *Both are okay.* The goal is **not** perfection—it's about showing up for yourself in ways that feel right *for you.*

Make It Your Own:

Choose what resonates with you—ignore what doesn't.

Some days, you might follow a structured routine; other days, you might go with the flow.

The key is **consistency**—small, loving actions every day create lasting transformation.

At the end of the day, **this is between you and you.** No one else. I'm just here to help.

Mantra: *"Self-love is not a destination—it's how I show up for myself every day."*

Final Thought

This **Self-Love Reset Routine** isn't about perfection. It's not about rigid rules or doing everything "right." It's about **choosing yourself daily** in ways that feel good, nourishing, and empowering.

Some days, self-love might look like deep reflection, journaling, or prayer. Other days, it might simply be drinking enough water, setting a boundary, or letting yourself rest without guilt. **It all counts.**

The most important thing to remember? **You are worthy of love—especially from yourself.** Every time you choose to care for yourself, in any way, you are reinforcing that truth.

You deserve the same love, kindness, and care that you give to others.

Now That We Are Finished: Self-Love Reflection

Just as we began with a **Self-Love Check-In**, we now take a moment to close this journey—not as an end, but as a continuation of something deeper.

Self-love is not a single act. It is not just routines or rituals. It is a **commitment to yourself**—a choice you make, over and over, in ways both big and small. Throughout this journey, you have planted a seed within yourself. Now, it is time to nurture it, to let it grow, and to recognize that this is only the beginning of a more profound relationship with yourself.

Take a deep breath. Sit with yourself. Reflect. Let these questions open the door to deeper self-awareness and appreciation for the person you are becoming.

Reflection Prompts:

- *What is one truth I've uncovered about myself that I didn't fully see before?*
- *How has my definition of self-love changed or deepened?*
- *What self-love practice felt the most powerful, and why?*
- *What patterns, thoughts, or habits have I begun to release?*
- *In what ways do I feel more connected to myself than when I started?*
- *How can I continue to honor myself, even on days when self-love feels difficult?*
- *What would my highest self say to me right now?*

This is not just about what you did during this reset—it is about what you felt, **realized, and awakened** within yourself. What shifted? What clicked? What parts of yourself feel softer, stronger, or more seen?

Reminder:

There is no final destination in self-love—only deeper layers to discover. There will be days where it feels effortless, and days where it feels like work. The key is to **continue showing up for yourself anyway**—not out of obligation, but out of devotion.

Because you are worth it. Every single day.

Mantra: *"I am not just practicing self-love—I am embodying it. I trust myself, I honor myself, and I will continue nurturing the relationship I have with me."*

What Does My Highest Self Look Like?

Self-love isn't just about healing who you've been—it's about stepping into **who you are becoming.** Your highest self is already within you, waiting to be embraced.

This is your chance to **define and visualize the fullest, most empowered version of yourself.** Not as someone far away or unattainable, but as the *real you*, without fear, doubt, or limitations.

Take a deep breath. Close your eyes if you need to. Imagine yourself **fully aligned, fully confident, fully at peace.** Now, let's bring that vision to life.

Reflection Prompts:

- *What does my highest self feel like?* (At peace, confident, radiant, limitless?)

- *How does my highest self move through life?* (What energy do they carry? How do they respond to challenges? How do they treat themselves?)
- *What are the non-negotiable standards my highest self upholds?*
- *How does my highest self practice self-love daily?*
- *What habits, thoughts, and environments support my highest self?*
- *What do I need to release in order to fully embody this version of me?*
- *What is one step I can take today to bring me closer to this version of myself?*

Aligning With Your Highest Self

Your highest self is not someone you have to chase or become—it is someone you **already are.** You activate this version of yourself **every time you choose self-love, every time you honor your needs, every time you refuse to shrink.**

You do not have to be perfect to be your highest self. You simply have to be **aware, intentional, and committed** to living in alignment with who you truly are.

Mantra: *"My highest self is not a dream—it is me, fully realized. I choose to embody this version of myself every day."*

Letter to My Future Self

Your journey **doesn't stop here.** The person you are today is **laying the foundation** for the person you are becoming. Growth is continuous, and this moment—right here, right now—is part of something much bigger.

Take this opportunity to **write a letter to your future self**, capturing the **love, wisdom, and clarity** you've gained on this journey. This letter will serve as a reminder of how far you've come and as encouragement for the path ahead.

Ideas for Your Letter:

Remind yourself of what you've learned about self-love, healing, and growth.

Encourage yourself to keep choosing self-love, even when it feels difficult.

Write about how proud you are of your strength, resilience, and the effort you've put into yourself.

Describe your highest self—how they move, think, and exist in the world. What does that version of you feel like?

Reassure your future self that no matter what happens, they are **strong, capable, and worthy.**

Speak with love and kindness, the way you would to someone you deeply care about—because *you* deserve that same love.

Bonus:

Seal this letter in an envelope (or save it digitally) and set a **reminder to read it in 6 months or a year.** When you revisit it, reflect on how far you've come and all the ways you've continued to grow.

Mantra: *"No matter where I am in my journey, I am always evolving, always learning, and always worthy of love."*

My Self-Love Commitment

Self-love is not just something we practice—it's something we **commit to.** It's a promise we make to ourselves, not just for today, but for the days ahead, including the hard ones.

This commitment is a declaration that **you are worthy of your own love, care, and devotion.** That your well-being matters. That you will continue to show up for yourself, even when no one else does.

Take a moment to fill in the blanks with what feels true for you. Let this be **your personal self-love contract**—one that you honor and return to whenever you need a reminder of your worth.

Fill in the Blanks:

I commit to treating myself with _____. (*Kindness? Patience? Respect? Love?*)

I will no longer tolerate _____ *in my life.* (*Disrespect? Overextending myself? Self-doubt? Negative self-talk?*)

I will prioritize my well-being by _____. (*Setting boundaries? Resting when needed? Speaking kindly to myself? Choosing joy?*)

I choose to believe that I am _____. (*Worthy? Enough? Strong? Whole? Capable?*)

When I struggle with self-love, I will remind myself that _____. (*I am always growing? I am allowed to be imperfect? I deserve love no matter what?*)

Let this be a **sacred promise to yourself**—one that no one can take away. Revisit it whenever you need a reminder of who you are and what you deserve.

Mantra: *"I am devoted to my own growth, healing, and happiness. I am worthy of the love I give to myself."*

Reminders for the Journey Ahead

Your **self-love journey doesn't end here**—it continues, expands, and evolves with you. There will be moments of clarity and confidence, and there will be moments of doubt and struggle. Both are part of the process.

As you move forward, keep these reminders close to your heart. They will guide you, ground you, and help you return to yourself when life feels overwhelming.

Take These Truths With You:

You are never starting over. Every step you take builds on the foundation of self-love you've already created. Even on tough days, you are still moving forward.

Healing is not linear. Some days will be easier than others, and that's okay. Growth is not about perfection—it's about showing up for yourself with grace, no matter where you are.

Your self-love practice will evolve. What works for you today may change over time. Let it grow with you. Stay open to new ways of caring for yourself as you continue to learn more about who you are.

You are allowed to take up space. You do not need permission to prioritize yourself, set boundaries, or choose what makes you happy. Your needs and feelings are valid. Always.

You are worthy of love, every single day. Not just on your best days, but on your hardest days too. Self-love isn't just for when you feel good—it's what carries you through when you don't.

Final Reminder:

No matter what, **you always have yourself.** You are your own home, your own safe space, and your own source of love. Keep nurturing that relationship, and watch yourself bloom in ways you never imagined.

Mantra: *"I trust my journey, I honor my growth, and I will continue to show up for myself with love."*

Acknowledgments

Writing this book has been a journey—one that wouldn't have been possible without the lessons, experiences, and people who have shaped me along the way.

To **every version of myself**—the one who doubted, the one who healed, the one who chose herself over and over again—thank you for proving that self-love is always worth it. This book is for you.

To **the readers**—whether you're just starting your self-love journey or deep in the work, thank you for picking up this book. I hope it reminds you of your power, your worth, and the love you deserve from yourself. I love every single one of you.

To **my closest circle**—the ones who have supported, challenged, and uplifted me, thank you for being real ones. Your energy, love, and presence mean everything.

And to **anyone who ever made me question my worth**—you played your role, too. Without those lessons, I wouldn't have learned how unshakable I truly am.

This book is a love letter to self, a celebration of choosing yourself daily, and a reminder that the best love story you'll ever have is the one you write with *you*.

About the Author

Bridgette Gajadhar is a writer, truth-seeker, and modern-day philosopher known for turning real life into real talk. Her work bridges the gap between clarity and action—pushing readers to think deeply, live honestly, and show up with intention. She's the founder of Pons Veritas, a platform dedicated to helping people reconnect with who they really are, what they truly want, and how to live a life that reflects both.

Born with a sharp mind and a soft heart, Bridgette's approach to personal growth is raw, empowering, and refreshingly unfiltered. She doesn't believe in fluff or performative positivity—only the kind of self-awareness that actually leads to change. Whether she's writing about purpose, ego, self-love, communication, or resilience, every word comes from lived experience and unshakable insight.

Bridgette's style is both relatable and revolutionary. She speaks to the overthinkers, the go-getters, the ones who feel everything deeply and still keep pushing forward. Her books don't just talk about healing and growth—they show you how to live it, day by day, moment by moment.

The Inner Clarity & Self-Mastery series is designed to help you stop settling and start living with intention. It's not about having all the answers—it's about finally asking the right questions.

To stay connected, visit www.ponsveritas.com and subscribe for updates, new releases, exclusive downloads, and a steady dose of truth you won't find anywhere else.

www.ingramcontent.com/pod-product-compliance
Lightning Source LLC
Chambersburg PA
CBHW071707120626
46550CB00001B/138